DIVINE
INTERVENTION

OTHER BOOKS AND AUDIO BOOKS
BY GARY W. TOYN

Life Lessons from Mothers of Faith

Life Lessons from Fathers of Faith

The Quiet Hero

DIVINE
INTERVENTION

INSPIRING TRUE STORIES FROM LDS SURVIVORS

COMPILED BY GARY W. TOYN

Covenant Communications, Inc.

Cover image *Surgeons in Operating Theatre* © Ivan Ivanov, Courtesy of iStockphoto.com, *Airplane Dog Fight* © Kris Hanke, Courtesy of iStockphoto.com, *Grizzly Bear* © Natalia Bratslavsky, Courtesy of iStockphoto.com, *Premature Infants Foot with IV* © AndyL, Courtesy of iStockphoto.com, *Climber Dangling From a Cliff Edge* © Greg Epperson, Courtesy of iStockphoto.com, *City Fire Department* © Jim Jurica, Courtesy of iStockphoto.com.

Cover design copyright © 2013 by Covenant Communications, Inc.

Published by Covenant Communications, Inc.
American Fork, Utah

Printed in the United States of America
First Printing: October 2013

19 18 17 16 15 14 13   10 9 8 7 6 5 4 3 2 1

ISBN 978-1-62108-567-6

CONTENTS

ACKNOWLEDGMENTS

MAYBE OTHER AUTHORS FEEL DIFFERENTLY, but for me, I am embarrassed to be singled out for the recognition that comes with writing a book. All books are the result of many named and unnamed people who contribute to the final product. Such is the case with this book. Permit me to recognize and acknowledge them for their efforts.

I first want to recognize all those whose stories are featured in this book, as well as those who assisted me in gathering vital information. They include the following:

Michael Dunn, who was kind enough to spend his valuable time with me to explain the details of his bear attack. It was also helpful to be able to listen to his fireside on CD, called *Bears and Prayers* (Covenant Communications). He not only tells a great story, but he offers some interesting and uplifting insights.

Megan Whatcott and her mother, Caren, for their willingness to share a very painful episode of their lives. I also want to thank J. J. Damin, and especially Jake Stockett for his help in providing photos and even video to help me visualize the steepness of the fall and of how difficult it was to rescue Megan. Megan's spiritual transformation after this episode remains among one of the greatest miracles of this book.

John Tippetts, whose patience and friendship I cherish. His inspiring book *Hearts of Courage* is the basis of our story "Determined to Endure." John spends a lot of time travelling and speaking about this event, and it doesn't matter if he's talking to an LDS gathering or a secular group, he always bears his testimony of how God answers prayers. I highly recommend his book, especially in commemoration of the seventieth anniversary of the "Gillam Crash" in 2013. You can find a copy of the book here: www.AlaskaAirMuseum.org.

Kathi Oram Peterson, who is simply amazing and a joy to work with. We met at a book signing some time ago, and she invited me to write for her blog KathisWritingNook.com. She has written many great books, and her heartwarming story in this book is further testimony of her skill as a writer. Thanks so much, Kathi!

Vern and Dorothy Stembridge. I was fortunate to have tracked them down long enough for them to tell me this story. I thank Lorraine Hoyt for telling me about them. Vern's simple yet powerful faith bears testimony of how willing God is to intervene on our behalf. Dorothy's faith, likewise, has much to do with Vern surviving. I appreciate both of them for helping me get this story put together.

Cheryl McLelland, the daughter of Theron Borup, who was kind enough to share her father's journal and other personal notes and photographs. Many others in the Borup family were helpful in getting the details collected, namely Myrtle Gallego, Carla Johnson, and Jane Amoureux.

Paul Oakey and his father, Alan Oakey, who were both kind and warm in sharing this amazing story. At the time I first contacted Alan, Paul was still recuperating from having his arm amputated. But both Paul and his father were open and willing to share this most personal and uplifting story.

Dan Liljenquist, who taught me a lot about the importance of obedience. He speaks reverently about this solemn experience, where several of his friends were killed. I not only thank him for sharing his story, but I was most appreciative of the deep spiritual insights he shared with me. He is a great example of the importance of making the most of each day we live on this planet.

Aaron Neal. After he ignored my request for almost a year, and I had almost given up on him. Then I found out he wasn't ignoring me at all: he was serving active duty with the army in Iraq. Once he got back to the States, he was very accommodating in telling me his story of being shot by a would-be robber. I thank him for sharing his story and for his service to our country.

Blake and Rachelle Knight, for having endured a great deal of anguish during the difficult aftermath of his brain tumor. I have noticed their spiritual growth as a result of this miraculous event. While their trials continue, I know they look forward to the time when they can say it was all worth it. Thank you for your faithfulness and for sharing your painful yet uplifting story.

Kitty de Ruyter-Bons, for giving us the basis of the story "A Mother's Love," which is based on her book *As I Have Loved You* (Covenant Communications). I have no doubt that she and her mother were spared by the miraculous hand of God. I thank her for her uplifting and inspiring story. I highly recommend her book. It's a great read, and you can't help but be moved by it.

Josh Holdaway, for allowing me to tell his amazing story about surviving a sub-freezing night in the Uinta Mountains. The circumstances of how he survived should be held in reverence, and I'm honored that he would share some of these very personal details with me. Josh is a good man, and it was great getting to know him.

Georgia Blanchard. I am so thankful I found her. We had a wonderful visit as she shared the story of her nephew Darwin Smith. She is a faithful woman who knows the historical significance of this story. It has been hailed as Mormon folklore simply because it is so amazing. If I hadn't held that Book of Mormon and seen the bullet hole myself, I would have also been skeptical. Georgia has been kind and patient as we have worked through the details of this story. I count her as a good friend and wish her and her husband all the best.

Matt Barkdull. He and I have been friends for over almost twenty years. His miraculous story is a powerful lesson in faith and patience. I'm glad he was able to see the lessons and was willing to share them. Matt is a gifted writer but was willing to allow me to write his story. I appreciate his confidence in me and for being a good friend.

Sara Staker, for her willingness to tell of how her son Bronson's heart stopped for nearly fifteen minutes. She was good enough to use her example to help others. Such selflessness underscores her goodness as a mother and as a faithful daughter of God. I also appreciate her ability to share her testimony of God's infinite love and mercy.

It has been a privilege to work with each of you and to be able tell your story in this book. Thank you again for your participation.

I must also thank the good people at Covenant Communications. Their talents and energies have blessed my life immensely and have also helped me grow as a person.

I especially want to thank Margaret Weber-Longoria for entrusting me with this project. It was her idea, and I take no credit for its concept. I am in awe of her creativity, as well as her patience throughout the long process.

I am likewise grateful for the ongoing support I've enjoyed from my direct contacts at Covenant. I'm especially appreciative for the trust and opportunity given to me by my good friend Ron Brough. It has also been a joy to work with editors Kathy Gordon and Samantha Millburn.

It was a privilege to work with my editor, Stacey Owen. She has been a tremendous help, offering inspiring insights and much needed encouragement. She has taken a very active role in writing and editing, but she has also helped me recognize the not-so-obvious spiritual lessons in these stories. She may be comparatively young, but she has wisdom and experience far beyond her years. She has been a joy to work with, and I hope we can work together again soon.

I am so thankful for my wife, Danita, for her love and confidence. At every step, she has offered her unwavering support, and I could not have finished this project without her. I love her, and I'm glad she is my best friend and eternal companion.

Most important of all, I must recognize and honor my Savior Jesus Christ. I count myself most privileged to be entrusted to write about these very sacred and spiritual events. He has given me everything, for I am nothing without His wonderful gifts, grace, and mercy. The blessings I receive from Him on an hourly and daily basis are infinitely far more than I could ever deserve.

PREFACE

As Latter-day Saints, we cherish the miraculous stories of the early days of the restored Church. Growing up, I was strengthened by the story of the seagulls eating hordes of crickets to save the crops of the pioneers and of the Mississippi River freezing just in time for the Saints to cross. These stories were told frequently and helped me come to a belief that "God has provided a means that man, through faith, might work mighty miracles" (Mosiah 8:18).

My interest in writing a book about miraculous survival was inspired by a highly personal experience in saving the life of my daughter. Through the power of the priesthood, I witnessed firsthand the manifestation of a higher law superseding a lesser law. This event was a milestone in my spiritual growth and led to tremendous growth in my personal testimony. When the opportunity was presented to start this project, the sacred nature of my miraculous experience gave me some serious concerns that I was "speaking of things I ought not" (1 Tim 5:13).

Those who witness or experience a miracle should rightly regard these events as sacred. Our latter-day scriptures have counseled us to take great care before discussing such spiritual manifestations openly: "Remember that that which cometh from above is sacred, and must be spoken with care, and by constraint of the Spirit" (D&C 63:64).

Through personal experience and after working on this project, I have come to believe that miracles are not so much about God arbitrarily reaching beyond the veil to intervene in our lives. Instead, I have come to the conclusion that He is constantly intervening on our behalf, and miracles are just a momentary glimpse of those ongoing blessings. We are allowed to witness these miraculous manifestations so our faith can be strengthened.

For reasons we don't always understand, God sometimes stays His hand, and miraculous events don't happen despite our righteous desires.

But we are promised in these instances that "if they die they shall die unto me" (D&C 42:44). For sometimes, as Elder David A. Bednar has taught, we need to have the faith not to be healed since not shrinking from our trials is often more vital to us spiritually than surviving (see CES Fireside, March 2013).

So are we, as Latter-day Saints, compelled to limit our testimony of miraculous experiences solely to the pages of our journal? Should all spiritual manifestations be spoken of only in hushed tones among close family members?

Frankly, I was greatly concerned about writing this book, fearing that I wasn't showing proper reverence for sacred events. It wasn't until Elder Jeffrey R. Holland spoke in the 2011 October general priesthood session, where he asked us as members to stop limiting ourselves and to be a stronger voice for good. It was like he was speaking directly to me when he declared that we should not be afraid to speak about miracles when we are guided by the Spirit (see *Ensign*, Nov. 2011). That statement was all the confirmation I needed to begin actively interviewing and writing the stories for this book.

But throughout the process, I have struggled to strike the right balance between the call to boldly speak miracles and the need to respect the sacred nature of these experiences. Fortunately, those who have agreed to participate in this project did so after much prayer and thoughtful consideration. Likewise, it is my hope that all who read these stories will be guided by the Spirit and will use caution when sharing these events with others.

Elder Dallin H. Oaks taught, "It is usually inappropriate to recite miraculous circumstances to a general audience that includes people with very different levels of spiritual maturity. To a general audience, miracles will be faith-reinforcing for some, but an inappropriate sign for others" (CES Fireside, 2000).

In appropriate circumstances, miraculous stories can be a mighty teaching tool and can inspire faithful people in wonderful ways. Some may read a story and be uplifted by the incredible nature of the events. Others, however, may glean powerful spiritual insights and can apply them to their personal lives. It is my belief that these stories can bless us all, whether we are lifelong Church members or new converts, whether we are just beginning our spiritual journey or farther down the path of discipleship.

Finally, I am grateful to everyone in this book who has shared his or her personal and sacred experience. After several years of work, I am blessed to have been inspired and guided to find these wonderful people.

I hope these stories can uplift and inspire you to greater faith and to a stronger testimony of God's love for His children.

OF BEARS AND PRAYERS
Michael Dunn

KEEPING HIS PACE UP, ABOUT seven-minutes per mile, Michael Dunn was lost in his thoughts. He was drinking in the bliss of the moment, surrounded by the stunning beauty of the Grand Teton National Park. It was an incredible experience, being alone with God's creations, wonderfully at peace and enjoying a seemingly effortless run.

Suddenly, his concentration was broken by the muffled sound of twigs and branches breaking behind him. Instantly, he thought of the animal tracks he'd seen earlier and unconsciously picked up his pace. His eyes strained to see into the undergrowth of the trees for the source of the commotion. The ground rumbled intensely, and he turned his head to look behind him. A massive brown creature was coming directly at him.

***

The morning of August 14, 1994, was simply stunning in the Grand Teton National Park. Michael Dunn and his family were at the end of their week-long vacation. They had traveled from their home in Park City, Utah, to the shores of Jackson Lake, Wyoming, to spend some time exploring the renowned landscape of the park.

Michael was training for the St. George Marathon, just six weeks away, so as he'd done each morning, he quietly gathered his shoes, clothes, water, and other supplies before tiptoeing out of the cabin. He tried not to wake his wife and three young children, who continued to sleep in their rented cabin at Colter Bay campground. Though he felt a little uneasy, this was his last opportunity to run before they left for home, and he wanted it to be a good one.

On the way out the door, he grabbed his sunglasses, though he wasn't entirely sure why. He hadn't used them on any of his previous runs that week, but it was a little later than normal, and maybe they would come in handy.

As he left the cabin, he glanced around enjoying the view. The sun hadn't quite peeked over the mountains, but its rays illuminated the jagged, rocky peaks, making it appear as though they were floating above the valley below.

Michael started the car and drove the few miles to the trailhead. After stretching his muscles briefly, he started at a slow jog before picking up his pace. Only a few minutes into his run, Michael noticed something on the trail up ahead. He found it unusual because the tall pine trees created a wall that shielded the trail from the sun's rays, but a small gap had allowed a beam of sunlight to peak through, and it illuminated the odd looking object on the trail.

As he approached the object, Michael realized it was a partially eaten pile of berries. He knew what that meant—a bear. His head shot up to see if he could find any signs of the creature. The paw prints in the muddy trail were unmistakable. His senses shot into overdrive. He listened carefully for any rushing in the bushes. After several tense minutes, he decided there was no immediate danger. If the bear had been nearby, it certainly would have been evident by then.

The tracks gave him pause. Should he continue to keep going? Should he turn back? His heart was saying, "Don't go," but his head kept saying, "You'll be okay. You can't afford to skip training." He convinced himself he'd be okay. There had never been a bear attack in the park before; why should he think there would be one now?

Though unsettled, he knew the first rule of avoiding bears—make noise. He began once more to run along the path, but now he was singing. He sang any song that popped into his head, and he sang it loudly. As the day grew lighter, however, he began to feel a bit foolish about his fears and stopped singing. He concentrated on his pace, mesmerized by the rhythm of his breathing and his feet striking the ground. He was grateful for the sunglasses as the sun's glare grew more intense.

Out of nowhere, he heard a loud sound behind him. He spun around only to see a huge bear closing in on him. It just was like the movies: time seemed to slow, and every detail was indelibly etched in his mind. He saw the unmistakable hump between the bear's shoulders and knew it was a grizzly.

The impact was powerful. Michael and the bear flew nine feet off the path, crushing nearby bushes. That was when the attack began in earnest.

Michael realized that the grizzly was intent on killing him. He tried to fight back. He didn't want to simply take the abuse without trying to get away, but his attempts were futile against the large creature.

The bear swiped its powerful claws across Michael's stomach and hip. Its front paw pinned his arm while it snapped its jaws at Michael's ribs and chest. With each bite it tore his flesh, gouging deep bite marks and puncture wounds on his back and shoulders. The bear's vicious attack seemed to go on and on. The pain became agonizing, and Michael hoped it would end quickly rather than leaving him helpless and suffering for hours.

A flood of thoughts rushed through his head. The first thoughts were of his two boys, ages ten and eight, and his little girl, who was just four years old. He gave each of them a mental embrace. Then his thoughts were drawn to his dear wife and all the heartache and grief she would endure. He hoped the park rangers would be kind in explaining his death. In his mind, he bid farewell to his family, hoping they would know and remember his unending love for each of them.

His attention was turned back to the continuing attack when one of the bear's massive claws caught the inside of Michael's mouth. Like a fishhook, the claw sunk deep into the soft flesh. The agitated bear tried to wrench its paw away, causing Michael's head to bend and twist unnaturally. Michael strained against the powerful force, and soon his muscles were shaking with fatigue.

When it seemed he couldn't resist any longer, Michael felt the pressure on his neck release as the bear's claw had come loose. Michael was once more lying face down in the dirt. The bear had now been mauling him for nearly two full minutes. Realizing these could be his last moments, Michael prayed.

"Heavenly Father, I need your help. I'm going to die."

Seconds after ending the heartfelt plea, Michael had an answer. Two words popped into his head—play dead. He instantly tried to follow the prompting. It wasn't easy—his heart pounded, the adrenaline surged, and his breathing was almost uncontrollable. He rolled over to his side as best he could with the bear still pinning his right arm, and he went limp.

Suddenly, the bear's attention was diverted. It was no longer aggressive and, in fact, appeared fearful when Michael peeked through his fingers to see why the attack had subsided. Seeing a window of opportunity to get the bear off of him, Michael swung a fist toward the grizzly's head. The creature was too large, and Michael's punch landed on the bear's arm.

Realizing his mistake, Michael once more played dead, but the bear hadn't even reacted to the ill-conceived blow.

The grizzly continued to ignore its prey, looking intently to the dense pine trees. It must have sensed something more threatening than the broken human beneath it. Michael felt the weight of the bear lift, and he took several deep breaths, refreshed by the uninhibited stream of air filling his lungs. He continued to lie still, barely daring to hope that the attack might be over.

Without further warning the bear began to scurry away. Michael felt the welcome sting of the dirt and rocks flung up as the bear picked up speed. It paused for a moment, rising up on its hind legs to survey the surrounding forest. Michael got a long look at the seven-foot-tall animal and marveled at the sudden turn of events. The bear acted as if it were in impending danger, turning and rushing into a thicket of trees.

Michael lay still for a few moments after the bear disappeared. He watched and listened closely, and when he was finally convinced the creature wasn't going to return, he tried to get up. His right arm and hand were too badly injured to support any weight, but somehow Michael managed to get to his feet. He was desperate to find help. He stumbled back toward the trail, dragging his right leg along behind him.

When he came to a small clearing, he paused to take stock of his injuries. He saw deep gashes in his legs and felt other gashes on his shoulders and head. Thinking remarkably clearly, Michael knew he needed to stop the bleeding to have any chance of survival. He pulled off his long-sleeved T-shirt and ripped it into long strips that he fashioned into bandages and tourniquets.

The adrenaline was subsiding, and the pain was becoming unbearable. His hands shook as he wrapped the strips around his thigh, arm, and head. Once he had done all he could to stop the bleeding, Michael stood once more and began to limp gingerly down the trail.

He knew he was at least ten miles from the nearest paved road, and since it was early, there weren't many people around yet. He hadn't passed a single person on his run, but he knew that he would not make it out of the woods on his own. His only hope was to find help. Digging deep within himself, Michael found the strength to keep walking.

Silently he prayed for help, asking God to guide someone to him. Minutes passed, and still the trail was deserted. Ten, then fifteen minutes passed, and he continued walking but was slowly losing strength. Stumbling along, he saw several trails ahead of him. He now had an important decision to make. Guided by an unseen power, he chose a path, trusting in the prompting he felt.

After nearly thirty minutes of this excruciating hike, Michael estimated that he'd only traveled about a mile from the point of the attack. He couldn't go any farther. He simply didn't have the strength to continue. He looked around for a place to lie down. It needed to be somewhat visible so that if anyone happened by, they would see him. When he finally collapsed on the ground, he did so wondering if he'd ever get up again. He knew he'd be found, but he didn't know if it would be a rescue or if they would only recover his body. His life was in God's hands.

Despite the blood loss and extreme pain, Michael never lost consciousness. Although he was growing increasingly dizzy, he expended the last of his energy screaming for help. For a half hour he screamed out, willing someone to hear and come to his aid, until finally he could yell no more.

***

When Michael didn't return as planned, his wife, Linda, knew something was wrong. Since Michael had taken the car, she was stranded with the three children, not knowing what to do. She decided they would ride their bicycles to the head of the trail where he normally started his run. As she readied the children, Linda could only pray that her husband was okay.

***

Over a mile from where Michael had finally lost the strength to go on, three photographers heard his faint yelling. Jim and Linda Bourett and Trisha Laving decided to investigate the distant cries. As they drew nearer, Michael heard their voices and gathered the remainder of his strength to call out once more. When they spotted him, the trio ran toward the torn and broken man.

They were shocked at the sight. Michael sat up among the undergrowth, his head, face, and legs covered with blood. His shirtless torso was sliced with deep wounds that continued to ooze blood. Dirt and dried leaves clung to him. He begged for their help, saying simply, "I was attacked by a bear."

The three rescuers consulted briefly and decided that the women would stay with Michael while Mr. Bourett went to find help. In his heavy hiking boots, he moved as quickly as possible back toward the road to find a park ranger.

The women did their best to tend to Michael. They gave him water, which he eagerly drank. They gently cleaned his wounds and picked away the dried leaves and dirt. They tried to offer what comfort they could.

Michael began to talk about his faith. He still didn't know if he was going to survive. He asked the women to make sure his family knew how much he loved them. The pain continued to grow more and more intense.

Almost two hours after the photographers found Michael and about three and a half hours since the attack, a ranger helicopter arrived at the scene. It was just before eleven o'clock when the paramedics lifted him onto a stretcher and the helicopter took off. Twenty minutes later, they arrived at St. John's Hospital.

Michael's wife and children eventually met up with him there. After an hour-long bike ride, Linda found a park ranger who informed her of the attack and drove her and the children to the hospital.

Doctors stood by to assess Michael's condition. Though wounds had been inflicted over his entire body, doctors identified sixteen major wound sites, all of which would require a great deal of stitches. They could still see the imprint of the bear's paw etched on his back.

His thigh was the most severely damaged. The bear had completely torn out portions of the muscle. Some of the cuts were so deep there was damage all the way to the bone. Remarkably, however, there were no broken bones.

The nurses began to clean his wounds, reaching deep inside to collect pine needles, bear fur, and other debris. Suddenly, one of the nurses gasped and extracted her hand carefully. The surgeon noticed the reaction and moved to her side to see what was wrong. She pointed out the femoral artery. It had been completely detached from the muscle wall, but was undamaged and still pulsing with blood.

The claws had missed on both sides of the artery by a mere millimeter. If that artery had been so much as nicked, Michael would have undoubtedly died within minutes. One doctor later told Michael that a surgeon with a scalpel could not have come any closer to the artery.

Doctors were equally amazed as they inspected the wounds to Michael's neck. The bear's claw had come only two millimeters from piercing the carotid artery. Dr. Paul Fenton, the orthopedic surgeon who worked with Michael, said, "Those claws can rip anything to shreds. How [that bear] never touched an artery is beyond me."

The whole scenario left doctors scratching their heads, wondering how Michael could have survived it all. In the randomness of a bear attack, it seemed so coincidental that all vital places were spared. They were also astonished that he could survive in the wilderness for hours, despite such major wounds, each of which could have taken his life. They repeatedly reminded him of how lucky he was, but Michael knew it wasn't just luck.

While he was still in the hospital, Michael received a visit from the park ranger investigating the incident. The ranger wanted to return Michael's sunglasses—the sunglasses he'd been prompted to wear that day. At the center of the right lens was a sizable dent obviously left by the bear's claw. If he hadn't been wearing those sunglasses, he could have easily lost his eye and probably his life.

Michael made a surprisingly quick and complete recovery. He continues to express gratitude to a loving Heavenly Father, who watched over and protected him that day.

LIFTED BY ANGELS
Megan Whatcott

AFTER AN HOUR OF CHALLENGING, technical climbing, Megan grew more concerned about making it to the top of the canyon. She carefully placed each step on the slippery white sandstone, making sure her footing was secure. With each step she grew more wary. Only the rocks and a few native juniper shrubs separated her from bottom of the gulch. Nervously, she looked up at the rim of the canyon. It seemed miles away.

Jake watched her anxiously from nearly thirty feet below. He offered suggestions as she negotiated the climb up the sheer mountain wall. She was now more than two hundred feet above the canyon floor. The canyon wall sloped at a nearly seventy-degree angle, and her foot was precariously gripping a narrow ledge.

"I'm scared, Jake. I don't know which way to go from here." She looked over one shoulder then the other, searching for a less tenuous foothold.

Jake knew she was in trouble. He saw the panic in her eyes. "Just stay there," he yelled. "I'll get above you, and we'll rappel down together." As he climbed, the two decided that Megan should remove the cumbersome backpack she'd been carrying. Doing so would increase her stability and decrease the strain on her shoulders.

Her foot nervously quivered, and Megan felt herself losing her grip. Though she had not prayed in a long time, she suddenly knew she needed to. *Dear Heavenly Father, please keep me safe!*

Suddenly, her foot gave way, and she was falling. Her terrified, piercing scream echoed through the canyon walls.

***

Megan loved the outdoors and took every opportunity to drink in all of nature's wonders. A few months earlier she had been working at the

Ponderosa Lodge, a large private resort adjacent to the park. That's where she'd met Jake. They spent their days off hiking and exploring the hidden slot canyons throughout southern Utah.

After the summer, Megan moved back to Salt Lake City. She was determined to have an apartment of her own and maintain her independence. She could have lived with her mother, Caren, but Megan was enjoying her new-found freedom. Best of all, with her own apartment, she didn't have her mom and her twin sister, Mandi, looking over her shoulder. And she could enjoy her hobbies whenever she wanted—including climbing with Jake in Southern Utah.

November 13, 2011
5:00 a.m.

They arrived at the Ponderosa Lodge around five in the morning. Megan had left her apartment early that morning. She didn't bother to tell anyone she was driving the five hours to St. George. Near Mount Carmel, her car ran low on gas. She stopped, but the gas station was closed, so rather than wait, she had asked Jake to come pick her up.

Jake had informed his supervisor, J. J. Damin, of his plan to rappel into Jolley Gulch with Megan. Jake had just purchased his own rappelling ropes and equipment and was eager to try them out.

12:00 noon

Jake and Megan set out, Jake carrying nearly thirty pounds of ropes, carabineers and harnesses, and Megan with a backpack full of water, smaller ropes, and other gear. Jake had also requested an emergency radio to take with them.

Because they were not permitted to drive into Zion National Park, the pair drove four-wheelers outside the park boundaries then hiked to the upper right side of the East Rim Trail. Carefully, they set their anchor and prepared their ropes to rappel into the tight slot canyon directly below them.

Reaching the bottom would require two separate descents—the first drop was about 160 feet and the second was another 100 feet. After two hours of cooperative work, they had completed the difficult descent. They enjoyed the sense of accomplishment at having conquered this challenge.

2:30 p.m.

It was time to head home. The easiest route back to the four-wheelers was a hike out of the canyon; however, it would take them nearly three hours to make that journey. The quickest way was to free climb up the canyon wall. Exhilarated by their recent triumph, the couple decided to climb the wall. It didn't look too difficult. They chose the path they would follow, and Megan led out.

After climbing only twenty feet, Megan realized the path was too difficult. She climbed back down and determined a new path. She and Jake found a new route, and she once again began the ascent. Over the next hour, the path grew more and more challenging. The uneven sandstone offered little by way of steady footing, and the higher she climbed, the more uncertain Megan grew. Jake tried to encourage Megan. He assured her she would be okay despite the steepness of the mountain.

3:30 p.m.

When Megan's pace slowed to a crawl, Jake knew this route wasn't working. He tried to calm and comfort her, telling her he'd climb up and rappel down with her. Suddenly, he heard Megan scream, and he watched, horrified, as she lost her footing. He bit his lip, holding his breath, watching helplessly as she fell.

"Please don't die, Megan. Please don't die," Jake repeated the words to himself.

There was nothing to slow her descent. She continued to fall feet-first, bouncing off the face of the mountain. Jake heard the sound of her hitting the wall echo through the canyon. He knew Megan had to have been severely injured, but she had fallen so far and so fast he couldn't even see where she'd landed. He scrambled to make his way down the mountain, screaming, "Megan! Megan! Are you okay?"

He got no response.

He pulled the emergency radio out to call for help. "This is Jake Stockett. Hello . . . ? Can anyone hear me?" No answer. He checked his watch. It was only three thirty; someone should still be manning the desk back at the Ponderosa Lodge. "J. J., are you there? Hello? Is anyone there . . . please . . ."

Finally, Jake heard J. J.'s voice, "I can barely hear you. Where are you?"

"We have a medical emergency," Jake exclaimed. "We need help immediately."

"Jake, this is J. J. Where are you?"

"Jolley Gulch. We finished our rappel and were headed out when Megan fell. She's not responding to my calls," Jake explained in desperation.

Suddenly, the radio went silent. Jake didn't spend any more time trying to reestablish contact. He had notified J. J. that they needed help and had told him where they were. Now it was time to find Megan.

Jake searched for the fastest way down, but he soon realized it was too steep. He would be no good to Megan if he was reckless in his rescue efforts. He knew his best option was to use his ropes to get to the bottom.

He wrapped his rope around a tree and began rappelling down the mountain. Every few minutes he called out, "Megan? Can you hear me? Megan?" He had no way of knowing whether she was even alive. Once he reached the bottom, he continued to call her name, but after five minutes of searching, he still hadn't found her.

***

J. J. knew the situation was desperate. He could tell from Jake's voice that whatever had happened was serious. He called the lodge office to notify them that they may need an ambulance and asked them to notify search and rescue officials.

Grabbing some rappelling rope and other gear, J. J. quickly packed an ATV and took off to find his friend. It was a twenty-minute ride to the rim of the canyon, and as soon as he arrived, J. J. began the descent. He only hoped he could find Jake and Megan before it was too late.

***

4:00 p.m.

Jake had searched for Megan for almost fifteen minutes before he finally found her lying motionless in a narrow slot canyon. Jake feared the worst. He ran toward her, calling her name.

Hearing him, Megan turned her head slightly and pleaded, "Please help me! I can't move."

Jake didn't know what to do. He felt helpless. He was a returned missionary but hadn't been attending church since; giving her a priesthood blessing felt wrong. But he knew the power of prayer, and he gently grasped her hands and spoke out loud. "Dear Heavenly Father, please bless Megan. Please bless that someone will get here fast. Bless her to be okay. Bless her not to worry and to be able to stay calm." It was a short but heartfelt prayer, and almost instantly, it brought tremendous peace to them both.

"We're going to get you out of here as soon as we can," Jake said firmly, trying to reassure the suffering young woman.

Tears welled up in her eyes as Jake inspected her injuries. Incredibly, she had suffered no head injuries, though she had not been wearing a helmet. Her shoulder was bent grotesquely forward and out of place. Her bloodied foot dangled precariously, nearly severed at the ankle joint. It was attached by only a small piece of skin and a few ligaments. The bone in her leg was exposed, and the wound was covered in dirt and sand. The pain in her stomach was so intense she didn't yet realize her ankle was nearly cut off. Tiny insects were soon attracted by the scent of blood and crawled on her congealed blood in the dirt below.

Megan had been resting on the cold, hard ground for nearly thirty minutes. The cool air and cold ground caused her to shiver. Jake realized that, besides the cold, she was probably suffering from shock. He pulled the emergency blanket from his first-aid kit. After wrapping it around her, he placed his jacket over her. She thanked him.

Megan was in a lot of pain and was anxious to find relief. She continued to ask, "When will someone get here?" Jake left her to walk down to the canyon and find a radio signal. He pressed for an update on the rescue effort, but he couldn't seem to get an answer.

Not wanting to discourage Megan, when he returned to her side, he lied, "They're coming; just hold on."

She tried to adjust her position to find a little more comfort, but she immediately grew frustrated with her inability to move. She could feel the pain in her misshapen shoulder and winced from the agony that resulted from shifting her hips slightly.

Jake didn't want to move her. He feared the risks of causing more damage if she had a spinal cord injury. He knew she needed help and urgently. She drifted in and out of consciousness, and Jake feared the worst.

"Stay with me, Megan," he would call out. "Don't go to sleep on me. You need to stay awake for me."

"When will I get out of here? How long is it going to take?" she asked repeatedly.

"They'll be here any minute now," Jake tried to reassure her, but in reality, he didn't know who was coming or when they would arrive.

Suddenly, Megan's eyes rolled back into her head. She began to convulse violently. Her head and upper torso twitched for several moments. Jake was frightened. It seemed the seizure would never stop. He was helpless as it continued unabated. For nearly two minutes, he could only watch until the convulsions stopped.

Fifteen minutes later she began to regain consciousness. Megan was not aware of what had happened, but she knew from the fogginess in her mind that something was wrong.

4:30 p.m.

Jake was relieved when he saw J. J. walking toward them. Megan had been lying on the ground for nearly an hour, and Jake was leaning over her, doing his best to comfort her.

J. J. was a trained first responder, but the only supplies he had were from a first-aid kit—adhesive bandages, sunburn spray—so there was little he could do. He assessed Megan from head to foot. Of greatest concern was her ankle. He tried to reposition the foot back where it belonged, but when he lifted it, it dangled loosely; he was afraid it would simply fall off. He did his best to wrap the bloody stump with gauze bandages to keep it clean. Incredibly, she had not lost as much blood from her ankle as he would have expected. It defied all medical logic; muscle tissue and blood vessels were visible. The lack of bleeding was a mystery.

J. J. made several attempts to use his radio to report on the situation, but the steep canyon walls made communication nearly impossible. Periodically, he hiked to a small clearing where he could get a better signal.

5:30 p.m.

J. J. learned that an ambulance had finally arrived at the canyon rim. Unfortunately, there was nothing the EMTs could do until search and rescue personnel delivered the patient. However, search and rescue had not received the message that they were needed, and so they were still not even mobilized. This confusion caused a serious delay in the rescue efforts. The clock was ticking, and her condition worsened with each passing minute. Finally, at five thirty, the Kane County Sheriff Deputy dispatched search and rescue.

When J. J. learned the ambulance personnel were not trained in rappelling, there was only one thing he could do: he had to climb to the top of the canyon to retrieve the medical supplies Megan desperately needed.

After thirty minutes up a shallow grade, he reached the top. J. J. gathered the supplies he thought he could use and prepared to descend once more. He asked for a quick lesson from the EMTs on placing a stabilizing neck collar and a splint for her ankle.

6:00 p.m.

It was almost completely dark by the time J. J. made his way back to Megan's side. With the sun below the horizon, a stiff breeze swept through the canyon. Megan shivered in the chilly wind.

Jake and J. J. built a wind break of whatever they could find—sand, rocks, backpacks. They were also able to make a fire with dead Manzanita bushes. It burned hot and gave off very little smoke.

The extent of Megan's injuries was still unclear, but she continued to complain of being cold so they knew they needed to get her off the cold ground. They devised a plan and dug a three-inch trench next to Megan, in the shape of the rescue basket. They moved the basket into place beside her and carefully lifted her. Using her uninjured arm and leg, Megan struggled to help slide herself into the basket. At long last, she was finally off the cold ground. She thanked them and soon began to feel the warmth on her back.

J. J. checked Megan's pulse every fifteen minutes. It continued to grow weaker. Her level of consciousness fluctuated, and she urgently needed fluid to replace the blood she'd lost. Jake voiced his frustration at how long the search and rescue team took to arrive.

7:00 p.m.

As Megan entered the advanced stages of shock, search and rescue medics Ryan McDonald-O'Lear and Brandon Torres arrived at the scene. They jumped into action, assessing Megan's condition. She complained of extreme pain in her stomach and shoulder, but she still didn't even realize her ankle was nearly severed. They could feel no pulse in the ankle, and it appeared that her foot would require amputation.

Megan's pulse was weak and erratic, her blood pressure dangerously low. She was in great pain, but pain medication was out of the question because of her blood pressure. She would just have to endure.

They worked quickly to start her on intravenous fluids then secured her in a rescue stretcher, or Stokes Basket. It took them nearly two hours to stabilize her for the trek out of the canyon. Jake and J. J. tried to distract Megan, but she complained about how long it was taking.

9:00 p.m.

Having immobilized Megan's body, J. J., Jake, and the two search and rescue medics latched on to a corner of the basket and began carrying her the half mile to where search and rescue had set up the hoisting operation. They selected an area that wasn't quite as steep, but unfortunately, that meant carrying her twice as far.

Lifting Megan up the hoist was slow, difficult, and dangerous. Inch by inch, three men pulled Megan up the mountain. The stopping and starting jerked Megan as she dangled. After ninety minutes of being jostled up nearly seven hundred feet, she finally made it to the top.

Once at the top, however, the ambulance was still a mile away. Search and rescue secured her to a cart specially designed to haul a rescue basket over rugged terrain. She was transported over a trail of sagebrush and rocks, experiencing jolts of pain with each bump and dip. After another painful thirty minutes, they finally reached the waiting ambulance.

The ambulance then delivered Megan to a medical helicopter, which flew her to Dixie Regional Medical Center in St. George.

12:00 midnight

Nearly nine hours after her fall, Megan was rushed into the emergency room. The nurses quickly cut her clothes away and assessed her injuries. There was severe bruising on her legs and arms. They also discovered a lacerated liver and spleen, which accounted for her loss of blood from internal bleeding and stomach pain. Her tailbone was broken, and other injuries weren't discovered until days or even weeks later.

Her shoulder obviously needed surgery, but her ankle was the most critical injury. Doctors could not find a pulse in her foot. The tissue, caked with dirt and grime, was swelling with infection. Before viewing the X-ray, the surgeon assumed her foot would need to be amputated, but the X-ray indicated her ankle was simply dislocated. Almost as soon as he re-set the ankle, blood again flowed to her toes. Yet several days later, doctors were still considering removing her foot when it continued to grow even more swollen and discolored.

Three days after the accident, Megan's mother asked the hospital staff to give her daughter a priesthood blessing. In the blessing, Megan was promised that she would return to full health. She was also informed that she had been protected because she had an important mission yet to fulfill.

Later, Megan and her mom finally had a chance to talk privately.

"I know I've been heading down the wrong path lately," Megan told her mother, "but I know this is a wake-up call for me." She also confided that while she was falling, she felt she was being lifted by angels. She recalled feeling as though she was being embraced as she landed and having a feeling of peace that everything would be okay.

She knew God had protected her in the two-hundred-foot fall. Incredibly, she avoided any head trauma or spinal injury. It's also amazing that she managed to fall feet-first, without tumbling head over heels. Even more curious, the doctors found no major scrapes or bruises on her back or hips.

"I know I should have died, and I don't know why I didn't," she admitted.

Likewise, Jake was astounded by her survival and recovery. "Surely, there is a reason why she didn't die," Jake stated. "Her life was in chaos before this event. She really needed to get back to her roots and embrace her faith."

Megan's recovery involved numerous surgeries and physical therapy, combined with faith and priesthood blessings. Today she has no limitations and can walk and run normally. She participates in almost all the activities she had done prior to the accident.

Megan's incredible survival had brought about a complete change in her life. In early June of 2012, she was called to serve as a full-time missionary. With a sparkle in her eyes, she looks back on this experience with gratitude for the support of family, friends, and a loving Heavenly Father, who sent angels to lift her during her fall.

DETERMINED TO ENDURE
Joe Tippets

ALASKA WAS AN INHOSPITABLE PLACE for a young widowed mother and her baby. It had been nearly three weeks since Alta Tippets had learned that her husband's plane had gone missing, and everyone had given up hope that there were any survivors. What did the future hold for her? Should she return to her family in Utah? Her only option was to ask God for guidance, so she got down on her knees.

***

Late afternoon of January 5, 1943, Joseph Tippets had been enjoying a much-anticipated flight home to Anchorage, Alaska. He had been in Utah visiting his critically ill mother, but he was ready to resume his duties as husband and father and as branch president of the Anchorage branch. His wife, Alta, had remained behind with their little boy, Johnny, to give Joe time with his ailing mother.

The flight had left Seattle, taking the coastal route toward Annette Island, the main refueling stop for flights going to Anchorage. At first, the weather had been pleasant enough, but as they traveled farther north, the blue skies turned to heavy clouds. Though the cause of the crash was never confirmed, it was suspected that increasingly cold temperatures caused ice to form on the plane until the left engine simply quit. The pilot used the radio to call for help: "One engine has conked out—expect trouble!"

Luckily, Harold Gillam was a veteran pilot intimately familiar with the harsh flying conditions in Alaska. In fact, "Thrill 'em, chill 'em, spill 'em, but no kill 'em Gillam" was almost legendary for having survived many close calls in his career—just the person to have in the cockpit during such an emergency. While speaking into the radio, Gillam glimpsed the fast approaching mountains and dropped the microphone to steer the plane over the oncoming trees. For nearly twenty minutes, he tried everything he could to stay in the air, but with the storm intensifying, impact was inevitable.

True to his nickname, though, Gillam managed to crash the aircraft into a thicket of trees, which prevented the plane from completely disintegrating and saved the lives of his passengers. All six people on the flight survived the crash with varying levels of injuries.

As Joe regained consciousness, he found himself practically standing on his seat. His head and upper body protruded from a hole in the plane's roof. A piece of glass from a window had been embedded in his seat, and had he not been thrust through the roof, he would have been impaled. He looked around to check on the others.

Percy "Sandy" Cutting had an injured back but was able to move on his own. Harold suffered from some internal injuries but could move about quite freely. Robert Gebo had a broken arm and leg. Any movement caused severe pain. Dewey Metzdorf had broken his collarbone and most of his ribs, causing numerous internal injuries. Susan Batzer was the most critically injured. Her arm had been pinned beneath some debris that had nearly amputated her hand.

Joe didn't know how long he'd been unconscious, but soon after he came to, he was overwhelmed by the smell of gasoline. Fearing the possibility of an explosion, Joe knew they needed to get out of the wreckage. He and Sandy teamed up to help the other passengers get free. It took them two hours just to extricate Susan. They laid her in the aisle of the cabin and attended to her wounds. She had lost a great deal of blood, and her condition was precarious.

That first night was long. There was a lot of time to think about the unlikelihood of their survival beyond a few days. They had little food, no shelter, and no medical care. Not only was it bitterly cold, the storm has not let up, so the survivors were wet and freezing. Frostbite would be unavoidable with the temperatures frequently dropping below zero.

The next morning, search planes inspected the nearby mountains where they had calculated they'd find the downed aircraft. Unfortunately, the plane had crashed near the top of a mountain, not near the water's edge as the would-be rescuers expected. Gillam shot several flares toward the planes, but they were never spotted. At one point, Joe watched the search planes fly at basically eye-level through the canyon. He could practically look into the cockpit and see the pilot fixated on the canyon below.

Another night went by, and the small group was no closer to being rescued. The next day they began to seriously worry about Susan. She faded in and out of consciousness. She thanked Joe for his assistance and attention through the past two nights, then she slipped back into unconsciousness. Susan died peacefully in her sleep. The men wrapped her body in a blanket and laid her to rest in the rear of the plane's cabin.

The rain and snow pelted them nonstop for four long days. Their business attire offered little protection from the cold or the precipitation. In the days following the crash, they had located their luggage. It was a blessing to be able to change into dry clothing, but the incessant rain kept them from staying dry for very long.

In an attempt to create some sort of refuge from the elements, Joe and Harold pieced together a cave-like shelter made from a wing of the plane and other wreckage. However, even with the help of gasoline, they were unable to start a fire in the wet conditions. They huddled close together to share body heat as they nibbled on rations from their diminishing food resources.

After a week of unbearable conditions, the weather finally cleared, and they could build a more substantial fire. It allowed them the first warmth they'd felt since the crash. As they dried out, they smiled and laughed with one another, feeling renewed and optimistic once again. The men also took advantage of the fire to dry out their extra clothes. Now they could bundle up in multiple, dry layers and stay a little warmer. Every little bit helped.

Joe put his shoes near the fire to dry them out, but he was momentarily distracted and the shoes were melted beyond use. His only alternative was to wrap his feet in rags.

Though Gillam had done everything he could to prevent the disaster, he felt a personal responsibility for their predicament. On the fifth day, he thought he heard an explosion. Hopeful it was a blast from the rock quarry on Annette Island, he set off to seek out help. Days passed, and the remaining survivors were forced to accept the fact that Harold Gillam would not return.

On the twelfth day, the planes stopped appearing. It was disheartening to realize that they had been given up for dead. The days dragged on, and it was all they could do not to despair. Idle time was spent in agonizing thought about all the things they may never experience again—the warmth of a loved one's embrace, the comfort of returning home at the end of the day, the taste of a favorite food.

To pass the time, Joe often read aloud from his book *Unto the Hills*, a collection of short sermons written by Richard L. Evans. The philosophical and religious topics sparked conversation and gave the men a meaningful way to pass the time. It was a source of inspiration and lent a peaceful spirit to their little camp.

This continued for almost three torturous weeks. They lived under the wing of the plane, sharing conversation and meager rations, waiting, hoping. One afternoon, Joe returned to the plane, desperate to find any morsel of food that had been previously overlooked. On his hands and knees he searched every inch of the plane—every inch except where they had laid Susan's frozen body to rest. He scavenged crumbs of bread, frozen grapes, and disintegrated apples—leftovers from the lunch they had eaten before the plane went down. These scraps were a feast for the four men stranded in the Alaskan wilderness. Their rations had consisted of the emergency supply of bouillon cubes, canned soup, and chocolate bars.

At one point they were able to shoot a squirrel with a rifle they'd found in the remains of the aircraft. They enjoyed the squirrel soup for five meals, completely finishing the creature, bones and all. They stretched the rations as much as they could, but as the supplies dwindled before their eyes, the men finally concluded that they would have to act if they wanted to survive. They needed to get off the mountain and into the valley, where the weather would at least be slightly more hospitable. They could see the bay in the distance and hoped that if they could reach it, they had a chance of being spotted and saved.

Robert Gebo and Dewey Metzdorf were still too badly injured to move, so Joe and Sandy fashioned a rough sled from one of the airplane doors to tote their friends to the bottom of the mountain. By the time they reached the bottom of the hill, their strength was spent. The men set up a new shelter next to the forest. It was decided that Robert and Dewey would wait in the makeshift camp while Joe and Sandy hiked toward the harbor looking for any signs of civilization in the vast wasteland.

On the night before leaving his two injured friends, Joe found a secluded spot to kneel and pray. "Heavenly Father," he pled, "I know my survival is a result of thy hand." He paused, then poured out his heart on behalf of his wife and family.

"Father, please bless and comfort Alta and give her peace," he asked. "Please let her know that I am alive and look forward to being with her."

It was a prayer of faith; he also felt at peace knowing God was in complete control.

***

Within hours of the time that Joe poured out his soul to his Creator, his wife Alta was doing the same. She needed the answer to a simple question: Was her husband going to return? Almost instantly, she received an answer, and for the first time since she'd heard the devastating news, she felt at peace.

Later that day, Alta received visitors. Members of her local branch had come to offer their support during this time of trial. They advised her to move home to Utah where she'd have the support of her family as she struggled to raise her son. Alta was certain that her husband would return, but she conceded that if they would give her one more week, she would begin to make plans to leave Alaska. One of the men, Mac McCarrey, remarked to his wife as they left the house that either Alta had completely lost touch with reality or she really had received some unmistakable revelation. No one could have predicted such an unlikely outcome.

***

Joe and Sandy set off to find help. It was a wild hope, but it was better than no hope at all. They trusted God to lead them, so they turned their backs to the camp and began toward the water's edge. They trudged through snow sometimes eight feet deep, stopping often to pull one another out of a hole. At one point they found a stream. They cut holes in the ice and tried to fish but didn't catch anything.

After two days of exhausting all their energy, Joe and Sandy arrived at the shore of the Boca Del Quadra Bay. Gathering a few logs, they attempted to build a raft, using strips of their last blanket to tie the logs together. They pushed the raft carefully into the water only to watch it sink before their eyes. They tried not to despair, but each attempt at progress seemed to end with discouragement.

Eventually, they happened upon an abandoned cabin. They found some salvageable food along with a rowboat and some tar to patch the holes. They patched the boat up as well as they could and climbed in to head across the bay to an old fish cannery only to find the entire compound abandoned. Desperate, they decided to risk the dangerous voyage into the open water in the hope of catching the attention of a passing ship.

It was not a good idea. Joe wrote, "The boat leaked almost as fast as we could bail. We bailed with one hand and paddled wearily with the other for about an hour. There was only one inch of space on the side of the boat above the water. After a couple hundred yards, we had to run the boat to shore and tip it over to empty it, and then start again." Unfortunately, things only got worse. A storm came up causing wind and waves. The boat capsized, and the two men were thrown into the frigid water.

For more than a half an hour, the men fought for their lives. Their clothing dragged them under the water; the waves dashed them against slippery rock then drew them back into the current. Eventually, they did make it back to shore, and they had been able to keep their matches dry in a tin sealed with tape. They warmed themselves by the fire, not knowing what more to do.

Starving, the two men decided to eat the tiny mussels they had found on the beach. They assumed that by doing so they would get food poisoning and die, but at that point it didn't seem to matter much—either die of food poisoning or starvation. With nothing to lose, they collected hundreds of mussels, and when the men survived the night, they ate more for breakfast.

The dawning of February second was just like any other day. It had been twenty-eight days since the plane went down. The men were losing strength and hope. But late that afternoon, Joe and Sandy saw the lights of a small boat almost six miles up the bay. The men expended the last of their energy to lug driftwood and branches into a pile and lit a bonfire. As darkness approached so did a snowstorm, and soon the fire had been extinguished.

Around five the next morning, the snow had slowed enough so the men could start another fire. By ten o'clock, they were too tired and discouraged to go on. They dejectedly returned to their camp.

Just five minutes later, they heard the most incredible sound—a boat engine. Joe and Sandy did everything they could to garner the attention of the crew, and finally they could see crew members waving back at them. Within minutes, the starved and frozen men climbed on board the *Tucson*. They hugged one another and cried in grateful relief that God had spared their lives.

The captain said they'd had no real reason to be in the area, but a new crew member had expressed interest in seeing the old cannery, so they'd headed in that direction.

Early the next morning, Joe and Sandy insisted on accompanying the coast guard search team to locate the companions they'd left behind. Thirty-one days after the crash, the last of the survivors were found barely alive. The men had given up hope of being rescued and had attached their ID cards to their hats to make sure their remains would be identified.

When the news reached Anchorage, pandemonium erupted. Men in the hallways of Joe's office wept unashamed. The women laughed and cried and hugged. It was an unexpected but joyful event.

The courage and faith of those men and their families had allowed them to live to tell one of the most incredible survival stories in the history of the Alaskan wilderness. But when asked about her husband's survival, Alta Tippets answered, "To me, it was simply an answer to prayer."

A SERVANT'S SURVIVAL

Lorenzo Snow

LESS THAN A MILE AWAY, the shores of Lahaina Harbor appeared serene and calm. The white-capped ocean roared as the small boat disembarked from the large schooner *Nettie Merrill*. The sea appeared safe enough to go ashore. From the vantage point of the ship, the passengers couldn't see the huge swells that menacingly rolled ashore.

The small craft contained an entourage of General Authorities—Elders William W. Cluff, Lorenzo Snow, and Ezra T. Benson were accompanied by former missionary and linguist Alma Smith—as well as Captain Fisher, several native Hawaiian passengers, and a small crew. Joseph F. Smith, later the president of the Church, had also made the journey, but refused to go ashore, waiting on board the *Nettie Merrill* for better conditions.

The boat moved slowly toward the shore, but the nearer it got to land, the more threatening the waves became. The passengers became increasingly nervous as the heavily loaded craft rose and plunged with the forty-foot swells. At one point they were lifted to such a height that the oars dangled uselessly out of the water. They were only a quarter mile from the beach, but suddenly they weren't sure if they would make it.

The captain's nervousness showed. "Hurry up! Hurry up!" he shouted with great alarm, but it was to no avail. The men at the oars were pulling with all their might, but the action did little to propel the group closer to the safety of the shore.

Chaos erupted. Another huge wave was forming, and this one would be their undoing. With a roar, it crashed into the boat.

***

After the Saints arrived in Utah, Brigham Young became one of America's most aggressive colonizers, founding over three hundred settlements in

Utah and the surrounding region. While there were many benefits to spreading out across the land, expansion was not without its difficulties. Political persecution, economic hardship, and a lack of leadership often threatened to overwhelm the small congregations.

In 1864, the Saints in the Sandwich Islands (Hawaii) were suffering from those very troubles. So when Walter M. Gibson approached President Brigham Young with a plan, President Young hesitantly agreed. Gibson, a convert of only a few years, offered to reestablish the LDS colony on the still-primitive islands.

Using a letter from President Young as evidence of his authority, Gibson claimed the leadership of the Hawaiian Saints, but it wasn't long before the faithful congregation began to grow suspicious. They noticed irregularities in how the Church was operated. One Brother wrote a letter to the prophet. In his letter, Jonatana Napela reported that Gibson was selling priesthood leadership positions. Gibson had also declared himself a prophet and required the Saints to bow to him. Unbeknownst to Jonatana and the rest of the Saints on the island, Gibson was also using the money he collected in the name of the Church to purchase personal property on the island of Lanai.

When Brigham Young received this troubling letter, he immediately dispatched a delegation to investigate. The journey was arduous and long, but these were serious allegations. A speedy investigation was essential. The entourage left Salt Lake City on March 2 and arrived at Lahaina Harbor on March 31.

The delegation was eager to get to shore. The trip had been long, and they had work to do. Even though two of the men had served missions in Hawaii and knew the dangers of navigating the reef, they finally agreed to undertake the short ride to the shore. A small boat was used to shuttle the passengers and cargo between the large schooner and the beach nearly a mile from where they dropped anchor.

The men climbed into the vessel, crowding around the heavy boxes and barrels filled with supplies. It was not long after they'd pushed off that they realized that it may have been prudent to wait for the ocean to settle before attempting a landing.

Finally, the boat could withstand no more pounding. At last, a monstrous wave crashed into them, littering the surrounding waters with oars, cargo, umbrellas, top hats, and passengers. The unforgiving waves pounded the bedraggled men as they bobbed helplessly in the water.

Elder Cluff had seen the big wave coming, and he dove into the turbulent waters. Worried at the thought of being struck by the debris, he swam a short distance underwater before surfacing. When he finally breached the surface, Elder Cluff immediately searched for his companions. Brothers Ezra T. Benson and Alma Smith had made their way to the capsized boat and were clinging to it. Captain Fisher had been swept farther away but was being assisted by two of his sailors. But Elder Lorenzo Snow, the future prophet and leader of the Church, was nowhere to be found.

***

When the natives on the shore saw the predicament, they immediately launched two rescue canoes. They rushed to aid the unfortunate travelers. One-by-one, the members of President Young's delegation were pulled aboard a rescue boat—all but Elder Snow, who was still missing.

Refusing to return to the beach, Elder Cluff insisted they continue the search for Elder Snow. He pleaded for the help of their rescuers. When they were certain the captain and others were safely on the way to the shore, the natives agreed to search awhile longer.

Several of the young men dove into the water. They searched in every direction for the missing man. Every so often, a young native would surface, shake his head in disappointment, take a deep breath, and slip back below the water. Time after time, they dove and surfaced, but still there was no sign of Elder Snow.

It had been nearly thirty minutes since their boat had capsized. There was little hope that *if* they found Elder Snow he would have survived. The intensity of the search waned. Sorrow set in.

At last, only one young man was continuing the search. He probed the ocean floor with his feet. Suddenly, he felt something. Taking a deep breath, he plunged beneath the surface. Within seconds, Elder Snow's dark hair was visible in the foamy seawater. Quickly, his lifeless body was dragged into the boat, and the natives rowed feverishly toward the shore.

Though Elder Snow was cold, blue, and still, Elder Cluff was convinced that it was not his comrade's time to go. He and Alma Smith held their friend's body on their laps. They placed their hands on his head and gave him a priesthood blessing.

The rescue boat jerked as it ran up onto the beach. The men climbed out, carrying Elder Snow across the sand. One of the large water barrels had drifted ashore, and, in a commonly accepted practice of the day, Elder

Snow's body was placed face down over the barrel and rolled back and forth. The combination of the pressure and the motion expelled the water from Elder Snow's lungs.

Many curious onlookers had arrived and watched the scene. Some tried to help. One man attempted to revive Elder Snow by washing the drowned man's face with camphor—another commonly accepted practice of the day. Nothing seemed to help. Seeing the hopelessness of the situation, many natives offered their condolences and began to walk away.

Elder Cluff, however, was determined. He continued to pray, asking for guidance and further assurances that his prayers would be answered. Finally, he felt inspired to try something else. Elder Cluff felt that he should try to imitate the natural breathing process, so he placed his mouth on Elder Snow's and blew hard to inflate the lungs. When the air escaped, he repeated the process. Mouth-to-mouth resuscitation was virtually unheard of at the time, yet Elder Cluff felt impressed to continue the process.

After nearly four minutes of this artificial breathing, a very faint indication of life returned to Elder Snow. After another minute, Elder Snow began to regain consciousness. Before long, he was breathing on his own. He coughed and expelled more water from his lungs.

Nearly an hour after the boat had capsized, Elder Snow was once more conscious, breathing, and talking. He later spoke of the experience: "Having been somewhat subject to faint, I think that after a few moments in the water, I must have fainted, as I did not suffer the pain common in the experience of drowning persons. I had been in the water only a few moments until I lost consciousness. The first I knew afterwards, I was on shore, receiving the kind and tender attentions of my brethren. The first recollection I have of returning consciousness was that of a very small light—the smallest imaginable. This soon disappeared, and I was again in total darkness. Again it appeared much larger than before, then sank away and left me, as before, in forgetfulness. Thus it continued to come and go, until, finally, I recognized, as I thought, persons whispering, and soon after, I asked in a feeble whisper, 'What is the matter?' I immediately recognized the voice of Elder Cluff, as he replied, "You have been drowned; the boat upset in the surf.'

"Quick as lightning the scene of our disaster flashed upon my mind. I immediately asked, 'Are you brethren all safe?' The emotion that was awakened in my bosom by the answer of Elder Cluff will remain with me as long as life continues: 'Brother Snow, we are all safe.' I rapidly recovered and very soon was able to walk and accompany the brethren to our lodgings."

The mission to reestablish correct authority on the island was eventually successful. Elder Snow's inexplicable survival is evidence to many of the Lord's power over the elements. The Lord had protected His servant, and under Elder Snow's leadership, the group helped prepare the Saints in Hawaii for the explosion of growth that would come in the following years.

NEWBORN WONDER

Kathi Oram Peterson

February 13, 1979
Riverview Hospital
Idaho Falls, Idaho

"Have you noticed your baby turning blue or having trouble breathing?" Concern creased the middle-aged nurse's forehead as she stood beside my hospital bed flanked by two student nurses. Riverview Hospital was training ground for Ricks College.

Shocked, I stared at her in disbelief. Seven years ago, I'd worked part-time on this floor as a ward clerk. Much had changed, but much had stayed the same. Many of the nurses I'd known back then had moved on to other jobs. This nurse, however, had been here when I had. Ours was a casual friendship. I knew her as Nurse Sarah. I'd seen her deliver bad news to anxious parents many times. I never expected she would someday do the same for me.

I stared at her, not wanting to accept what she was saying. She was supposed to bring my son to me so I could dress him to go home. I glanced down on my bed. A warm bunting waited to shield my little boy from the bitter cold of this wintry day. I'd looked forward to dressing him in the bunting and wrapping him in the soft blue quilt I'd made two babies ago but hadn't used because we'd had girls. Only a couple of hours had passed since Nurse Sarah had told me she was in love with my son, Benjamin. I was in love with him as well. I'd shared with her that I'd felt as though I was living a dream. I had two adorable little daughters and now a beautiful son. He was three days old, and many times as I'd held him, I felt as though he might vanish from my arms. Now, Nurse Sarah and her students stood beside my bed wanting to know if I'd noticed my baby not breathing.

My nightmare had become real. Prickles of fear bristled as I tried to remain calm. "When I fed him earlier, he was okay. What's wrong?"

"He's stopped breathing several times. We've revived him. Dr. Wilford is examining him now, but if you'd like, we could call another pediatrician." She watched me, waiting for me to say something.

Tears clouded my vision. I knew Dr. Wilford was one of the best. "I don't have a pediatrician. My doctor is out of town. Dr. Wilford will be fine." My husband and I had decided not to go the specialist route and had chosen a general practitioner to deliver our baby and take care of both me and the infant. However, I had delivered early, and my doctor was out of town, so Dr. Burns, another GP, had delivered our son. Everything had gone well. But now, *everything* had changed.

Before leaving, Nurse Sarah leaned over and gave me that hopeful but cautious smile I'd seen her give others many times. She said, "We're doing everything possible." And then she and her students left.

I grabbed the phone and called my husband, Bruce. The line was busy. Of all times for the phone to be busy. Again tears threatened, but I ignored them. I dialed the operator. She immediately answered.

Images of my beautiful son and the words "stopped breathing several times" jammed my thoughts. My tongue swelled as I tried to form the necessary words. Finally, "My line is busy, and I need to speak with my husband right away."

"Are you calling from the hospital?" The concern evident in her voice comforted me.

"Yes."

"One moment, please." And she was gone.

The next voice was Bruce. "What's wrong?"

I told him what had happened. We lived several miles north of town on the west bank of the Snake River, so it would take time for him to get to the hospital—time I didn't know if our son had. Bruce said he'd pick up my brother, Bill, on his way so they could give Benjamin a blessing. Then he was gone, and I was alone . . . again.

I hung up, remembering the times I'd watched other terrified couples standing at the nursery window watching as doctors and nurses battled to keep their newborns alive. Many babies lived, but many died. The tears that I'd fought before welled in my eyes, ran down my cheeks, and dropped to my chest. In that moment, I knew that even with the best medical help Benjamin could still die, still vanish from my life if it was the Lord's will. Feeling helpless, I turned to my Father in Heaven and poured my heart out to Him, begging for my son's life in a silent prayer.

The head nurse from the nursery came in. I didn't know her. I wiped tears from my cheeks.

She put her arm around me. "Do you want to see your baby?"

Of course I did. Instead of answering, I just eased out of bed, stitches from the episiotomy still tender. She walked with me down the hall to the nursery. Before going in, I had to wash with Betadine and slip a sterile gown over my pajamas. At last, I stood beside the incubator where Benjamin struggled for breath. A heart monitor had been taped to his small chest. Here was my perfect baby. Ten tiny fingers. Ten tiny toes. Dark, thick baby hair covered his little head. Even as small as he was, he looked like his daddy. The only visible problem: the struggle of his rib cage as it rose and fell. I wanted to scoop him into my arms and tell him I loved him and that everything would be all right.

But I couldn't. Glass separated us. The life-sustaining air from the incubator had to cuddle him for now. I don't know how long I stood there, staring at my son, willing him to keep breathing, but I eventually noticed the nursery seemed quiet. The nurse was no longer by my side.

Glancing through the nursery windows, I saw that Bruce and Bill had arrived. Bill was taking off his muddy coat and boots. I wondered briefly what he'd been doing. They scrubbed their hands, put on gowns, then came into the nursery.

The head nurse pulled a rocker close, motioning for me to have a seat. She opened the incubator, disconnected the heart monitor, and handed me my son. I cradled him in my arms and stroked his soft skin. Bruce and Bill laid their hands on Benjamin's head and gave him a blessing. Listening to every word, I hoped to hear that my baby would overcome this illness. But instead I heard, "If it be thy will." Though I knew everything in life was according to the Lord's will, I wanted my son to live.

Benjamin's skin turned blue. He'd grown limp. The blessing ended, and the nurse quickly took him from me, returned him to the incubator, and reconnected the heart monitor. I stood watching the machine recording my child's heart rate. It was below one hundred.

"What's a normal heart rate?" I asked the nurse.

Adjusting the oxygen level, she glanced at me and said, "One-twenty."

I could tell by the look in her eyes that she, too, was worried.

A portable X-ray machine arrived. They took shots of my son and then left. Now the waiting began. I continued to gaze through the incubator, willing my baby boy to keep breathing, willing his heart to keep pumping.

A nurse came and told me that my lunch was waiting in my room and I should try and eat something. Bruce assured me that he'd stay with Benjamin. I didn't want to leave, but I knew I had to keep my strength up, so I could nurse my baby when he was well again . . . if he was well again.

I reluctantly went back to my room, ate what I could, then returned to stand vigil. As I began to scrub before entering, the head nurse stopped me. Bruce was with her. She picked something up from the counter and said, "The X-ray department called with Benjamin's results."

I looked at Bruce. He stared back at me. We were both eager to know yet scared to death. Bruce wrapped an arm around my shoulders, and we stood side by side waiting to hear.

"Benjamin aspirated and has milk in his lungs. We need to move him into the Intensive Care Nursery. He will be there for at least a week. We may have to feed him with a tube through his belly button." She pointed to the paper in her hands. It was a chart showing how that worked. She looked at Bruce. "Why don't you take your wife back to her room while we get Benjamin resettled?"

Bruce nodded, and we made the long walk down the hall away from our baby. I realized that my brother was no longer with us. "Where's Bill?"

"Gone home." Bruce looked straight at me. "The strangest thing happened when I stopped to pick him up at the new house."

Bill and his family were living in our parents' house while Mom and Dad were on a mission in Columbia. Bill was building a new house down the street from ours, and he was anxious to get it done because our parents would return in less than a month. Mom and Dad were anxious to meet their new little grandson and had surprised us all with the news that they could come home a month early.

Bruce continued, "I stopped at the new place, but I couldn't find him. I looked around the house and in the back, but there was no sign of him. As I was getting ready to leave, I heard someone calling for help. I realized the voice was coming from a deep hole near the road. I ran over and found Bill trapped inside. A water main had frozen, and he'd been trying to thaw it when he'd gotten stuck. Pulling him out, I hurried him to the car, telling him about the situation at the hospital. Bill wanted to change his muddy clothes, but I told him there wasn't time."

"So that's why his coat was muddy." I marveled that in our crisis my husband was able to help my brother out of a dangerous situation. "What would have happened if you hadn't come along?"

Bruce shrugged. "There's no telling. The subdivision is fairly new and rural. Not many people are out and about in this cold weather."

We realized that my brother easily could have frozen to death. How many miracles could we expect from the Lord this day? I prayed for one more. Please, just one more. Was I being selfish? No! I wanted Benjamin to come home with me. I wanted everything normal again.

We walked down the hall in silence. Once I eased into bed, Bruce told me he needed to run some errands. He wanted me to get some sleep. I knew he was worried, so I told him to leave, and I'd take a nap. He was concerned because when I'd given birth to each of our daughters I'd had a problem with hemorrhaging a couple of days after. He didn't want there to be any additional problems.

As soon as he left, I pulled the privacy curtain around my bed and said another prayer. I don't know how long I prayed, but it must have been awhile because not long after I finished, Bruce returned, and we went to the Intensive Care Nursery to check on our son. Nurses constantly monitored him. Machines pumped. Lights flashed. Benjamin's future seemed bleak.

Afternoon drifted into evening with my husband and me making many trips to peer through the nursery window. Eventually, Bruce had to go home to relieve the babysitter and check on our daughters.

Close to nine that evening, the night-shift nurse came to my room. "Do you want to feed Benjamin?"

For a moment, I was worried. Maybe this nurse wasn't thoroughly briefed on his condition. "I thought you were going to feed him through his belly button."

She smiled and said, "That's a last resort."

Hopeful, I asked, "Can I nurse him?"

"No, but you can give him a bottle." She helped me out of bed and took me to the nursery.

After scrubbing and putting on a sterile gown, I followed the nurse into Intensive Care. She'd already positioned a rocker near Benjamin's incubator. She opened the lid, and being especially careful of the many wires taped to him, she wrapped him in a warm blanket and handed him to me. Holding my precious child in my arms, I gave him the small bottle of milk. He hungrily drank. When he finished, I burped him, watching him intently in case he choked. As soon as he burped, the nurse placed him back in the incubator. Reluctantly, I went back to my room but couldn't sleep.

At six a.m., I returned to the nursery. The morning crew had come on duty. A cheerful and rested nurse said, "After you fed your baby, he had a good night. Do you want to try nursing him?"

"Yes!" I quickly scrubbed, donned the sterile gown, and followed her to Benjamin. She took off the wires taped to him, wrapped him in a blanket, and handed him to me. She'd turned the rocker away from the nursery window, and as I prepared to feed him, she thoughtfully draped a blanket over me for cover, leaving a gap so I could watch my son.

Afterward, as the nurse returned him to the incubator, she said, "He's much improved. It's as though he's never been ill."

I was very encouraged, raced back to my room, and called my husband.

Bruce's groggy voice answered, "Yeah?"

"Benjamin had a good night. You've got to see him."

"What?"

"He's better!"

"Really?" Now he was fully awake. "I'll be there as soon as I can find a sitter."

Minutes seemed like hours as I waited not only for Bruce but for the doctors to examine Benjamin. I knew that Dr. Wilford and Dr. Burns did rounds between eight and nine each morning, so at eight, I made my way back to the nursery and found Dr. Wilford on the phone. I stood near the door, anxious to speak with him. He motioned for me to have a seat.

Hanging up, he turned and said, "I was just verifying the lab results. I can hardly believe this, especially after yesterday, but Benjamin's lungs are clear."

"Clear?"

He nodded. "Checked twice. I see no reason why you can't take him home today."

I thought of the chart the nurse had shown me of feeding a baby through the belly button; I thought of the week that Benjamin was supposed to stay in the hospital; and then I thought of the blessing Bruce and Bill had given my newborn son. Excitement coursed through my body. I wanted to sing and dance and shout. Instead, I shook the doctor's hand and said, "Thank you!"

Elated, I returned to my room and called Bruce. I caught him before he'd left. "The doctor said we can take Benjamin home today."

He was quiet for a moment. Finally, he said, "Are you sure?"

"Yes! Hurry and come get us." I hung up.

As I prepared to leave the hospital, Nurse Sarah entered my room with the same two student nurses from yesterday by her side and with Benjamin in her arms. She helped me dress him. The newborn diaper and T-shirt looked huge on his little frame. I quickly put him in the warm bunting.

Nurse Sarah stood, watching me with a huge smile on her face. She said, "You know, don't you?"

"Know what?" I asked.

"You're holding a miracle?"

Smiling back at her, I thought of the other people I'd seen years ago, those Nurse Sarah had given bad news to. This woman had seen both death and life. She knew a miracle when she saw one.

And now, so did I.

DIVIDED ASUNDER

VERN STEMBRIDGE

VERN POINTED AND HOLLERED AT the driver. There was excess gravel accumulating near the paving machine, and that could cause problems if it wasn't removed quickly. He'd found the driver and was shouting, trying to get the man's attention. It was too loud at the construction site, and Vern finally gave up, realizing he would just have to walk over and talk to the driver. He was so focused on this task that he didn't see the dump truck operator backing up. The truck struck Vern with such force that he flew over five feet in the air.

***

Sixty-year-old Vern Stembridge was the construction inspector on the major road-paving project outside Park City, Utah. He had been on the job for about thirty-five years, rarely missing a day. As the construction inspector, Vern was responsible for overseeing the work site. He ensured that the host of laborers and the machinery were all performing their jobs properly. If he found irregularities or problems with men or equipment, he had the power to shut down the project immediately.

This particular project had presented some additional challenges. The intense July heat was stifling and tried the workers' patience. The miserable conditions were made almost unbearable by the added heat of the oil and engines throughout the site. Most of the men were eager to get the job done as quickly as possible and then find relief from the sweltering day. Without a good inspector like Vern, some might be tempted to get careless or take shortcuts that could lead to disastrous consequences in the future. Vern knew he needed to pay close attention.

On this day, the project was nearly three-quarters completed. One lane was done, and they were working on the second, anxious to finish. It needed to exactly match the grade of the pavement they had laid the week before. Vern watched now as they prepared the gravel base to lay the new pavement. They sprayed the base with hot oil so that the pavement would adhere to the road base. Vern's job included making sure the oil was at the proper temperature. If it was too hot or not hot enough, the pavement wouldn't stick.

This morning Vern had checked the oil's temperature—255 degrees Fahrenheit. That was a little hotter than normal but still well within the acceptable range. Vern watched for a moment as the men sprayed the gravel. Satisfied with their work, he walked around the oil truck to make some other observations. That's when he noticed the gravel accumulating near the paving machine. He had to walk around an idling asphalt vehicle, two dump trucks, and numerous other machines before he found the driver; but the machinery was too loud, and Vern couldn't get the man's attention from so far away.

Vern stepped onto the hot asphalt, and the next thing he knew, he was flying through the air. He landed on his stomach directly on the scorching oil that had just been applied. Dazed and in pain, Vern tried to stand, but he couldn't move. The oil was burning his skin, but Vern lay helpless, watching the dump truck drawing closer.

He instinctively put up his hands, futilely attempting to stop the vehicle from running him over. It was like watching a tsunami rush toward him and knowing there was nothing he could do to stop what was about to happen. As the forty-eight-ton truck made contact, Vern began to scream in agony, but his cries were barely audible above the clanking of the machines and the roaring of the heavy-duty construction vehicles.

A few men noticed Vern lying on the ground, and they added their voices to the shouts for the driver to stop. "Stop! Stop!" The driver couldn't hear anything, completely oblivious to the commotion that was now taking place at the rear of his truck. Finally, glancing in his rearview mirror, the truck driver noticed a crowd of men scrambling. Something was clearly wrong.

The driver slammed on the breaks, and the truck lurched to a halt. Suddenly, a foreman ran to the cab, jumping up to the driver's side window. "Don't go back any farther." The words tumbled out quickly, urgently. "You've run over the site inspector. We're going to move you forward slowly."

Directed by the same foreman, the driver inched his vehicle forward off Vern's broken body. The truck had stopped at just the right moment.

Had it gone mere inches farther, Vern's heart would have been crushed, and he likely would have died instantly. As it was, Vern's leg had been pressed into the pavement. The wheels had crushed his upper leg, hip, and torso nearly to his sternum.

Vern's skin had also been torn from the sheer weight of the vehicle. It was a gruesome sight. His internal organs were exposed to the hot oil, gravel, and asphalt. Vern drifted in and out of consciousness. He pleaded for help and relief then blacked out once more. After several tense moments, the wheels were finally off Vern, but the damage was severe.

In another moment of consciousness, Vern begged a coworker to get a coat from Vern's truck. The hot oil seared Vern's skin like fire. He wanted something underneath him to relieve the burning.

Despite the isolated and distant location, paramedics arrived on scene within minutes. It was obvious that Vern's chances of survival were slim. Pushing aside their doubts, the paramedics sprung into action, dressing his wounds and working to keep Vern from going into shock. They were surprised that he didn't seem to have lost much blood. Apparently, the hot oil had cauterized some of the wounds. It temporarily kept Vern from bleeding excessively.

Immediately upon seeing Vern, the medics knew that there was no way they could get him to a hospital in time. They wasted no time in calling for a medical helicopter, but even then, they didn't know if Vern would make it to the hospital. Typically, the helicopter would take twenty to thirty minutes to even arrive on the scene, but someone was watching over Vern.

The University of Utah AirMed helicopter had taken an unexpected and unscheduled flight to Heber City and was now virtually above the accident site. In minutes, the aircraft had landed and loaded Vern inside. As soon as he was safely strapped in, the helicopter lifted off. Vern was shaken back into consciousness by the turbulence of the rotors as the craft left the ground. He wasn't conscious for long. Suddenly, the heart rate monitors blared loudly, no longer detecting a heartbeat.

The medical team worked quickly to remove what remained of Vern's shirt. They administered a shock with the defibrillator. Vern's body jerked from the shock, and his heart began to beat once more.

During the ten-minute flight to the University of Utah hospital, Vern's heart stopped five times. Incredibly, only eighteen minutes had passed from the moment he'd been hit to the moment he passed through the doors of the emergency room.

***

As doctors scrambled to save Vern's life, others worked diligently to contact Vern's family. With access to a public safety database available only to police, officials attempted to contact his wife, Dorothy. They could not reach her or anyone else in the family who might know how to get in touch with her. They contacted a former employer, then dispatchers tried to contact Vern and Dorothy's son-in-law, Kurt, who lived about forty minutes from the hospital.

Kurt wasn't home, but he had left his number with the babysitter, something he didn't typically do. Fortunately, they were able to reach him, and he immediately rushed to the hospital. Kurt arrived a half hour after his father-in-law. While doctors and nurses worked around them, Kurt and a hospital employee gave Vern a priesthood blessing. It was brief but very powerful. Though survival seemed unlikely, Vern was promised that he would fully recover.

Shortly after the blessing, Vern began to bleed profusely. The blood came from his abdomen and legs without warning. Working fervently to stop the bleeding, the medical team tried everything. As they applied pressure to the wounds, Vern cried out in pain. The doctor ordered an injection of Propofol, a short-acting drug that would induce a coma-like state so Vern would not have to feel the excruciating pain of the treatment.

They continued trying to staunch the flow of blood, beginning a transfusion in his arm. His blood pressure continued to fall, and when it was clear one line wasn't enough, they inserted another needle into his jugular vein, allowing for more blood to flow into his body. Still, they couldn't stop the bleeding.

Out of options, doctors elected to attempt an experimental procedure. They would surgically insert Styrofoam-like plugs in some of the affected veins. The plugs would expand when they came in contact with the blood and would theoretically slow the bleeding. After a few tense hours, the procedure had been completed and appeared to have been successful. They had somehow stopped the bleeding, but in the process they had used fifty-five pints—nearly fourteen gallons—of blood.

***

After kissing her husband good-bye that morning, Dorothy finalized her plan for the day. She was looking forward to a fun day at Lagoon, a popular amusement park, with some of her extended family.

By eleven o'clock, she was inside the gates, waiting for the rest of the family to arrive. While she waited, Dorothy decided to go change into her swimsuit. Perhaps she'd run into her sister at the pool.

She headed toward the locker rooms, enjoying the warmth of the sun and listening to the growing sounds of enjoyment in the park—playful screams, lifeguards' whistles, children's laughter. Suddenly, she stopped. Had someone called her name?

Pausing outside the locker room doors, she strained to hear the announcement over the loudspeaker. "Dorothy Stembridge, please go to the Lost and Found area." She waited for any sort of explanation, but none came. A little stunned, she began to make her way to the Lost and Found. She picked up the pace as she realized that something must be wrong. In a near-panic, she approached a couple of employees and asked for directions to the Lost and Found desk.

When she finally arrived, she identified herself to the attendant, who handed her the telephone. It was a doctor from the emergency room at the University of Utah hospital. He explained that her husband had been in an accident and that she needed to get to the hospital immediately.

Horrified, Dorothy hung up the phone, thanked the teenager behind the desk, and spun around toward the exit. The attendant eyed her carefully, concerned at her reaction to the news. She was clearly shaken, but she gathered herself together and made a beeline for the exit.

Dorothy moved as quickly as she could toward the parking lot, but as she neared the gates she thought of trying to get to her car. She had parked on the fringes of the parking lot now crammed with buses, RVs, minivans, and cars. It would take some time to find her car in the sea of vehicles.

Determined to get to the hospital, she continued unfazed through the turnstile. She pointed herself in the direction of her car but barely made it a few feet before running into her sister's family on their way into the park. Dorothy quickly rehearsed the news. She followed her sister and brother-in-law to their nearby car and started south.

***

While the medical staff worked to stop the bleeding, the doctor had instructed that Vern receive an injection of Propofol. This highly utilized medication renders 96 percent of patients unconscious. Unfortunately, Vern was in the minority when it came to the effects of the drug. The medication temporarily paralyzed him, leaving him helpless to respond to pain or communicate with doctors. To onlookers, he appeared to be unconscious, but in reality, he felt every ounce of pain.

Doctors and nurses cleaned wounds, inserted needles, and peeled away tissue covered in oil, gravel, and asphalt, oblivious to the pain they were causing their patient. When the doctors realigned his broken ankle bones, Vern felt white-hot pain caused by the pulling and twisting of the bones. The drug had paralyzed him, though, so there were not even involuntary movements, pained expressions, or rapid breathing to hint at his state of consciousness.

Second and third degree burns covered nearly forty-five percent of Vern's body. There were gravel and asphalt particles imbedded on most parts of his stomach and legs. The nurses began to debride his burns, a process of scrubbing away dead and contaminated tissue to aid healing. They scrubbed, picked at, and rinsed the wounds. For all they knew, Vern was comatose, unable to experience any pain. Vern could do nothing but endure.

***

When Dorothy arrived at the hospital, she saw hordes of people scurrying in and around Vern's room. Tears flowed freely as she helplessly watched the staff working on her apparently comatose husband. She was shocked at the amount of blood and the number of discarded bandages littering the room.

She was approached by a nurse, who asked if Dorothy was related to Vern. Dorothy explained she was his wife. The nurse summoned a doctor, who explained the situation and warned Dorothy that the prognosis was not good. Trying to prepare her for the likely death of her husband, the doctor told Dorothy that they did not expect Vern to survive the night. He couldn't even tell her the extent of the damage, though, because they were still trying to get Vern medically stabilized.

Trying to make her understand the probability of Vern's death, the doctor pointed to her husband's lower legs, visible between the staff who still stood over Vern. Although Vern was technically alive, the physician explained, the death process had already begun. Hypostasis, the setting of solid particles in the blood, had left a purplish-red discoloration from his knees down to his feet. And while the staff worked diligently to save his life, many of them believed there was no way Vern would survive. It was really only a matter of time.

For twenty-four hours, Dorothy remained at her husband's bedside. The powerful emotions she experienced left her drained. She felt as though she'd been kicked in the stomach. But she also found a small glimmer of hope. The doctors had told her that Vern wouldn't survive the night, but he had. He had even stabilized and been moved to a burn unit.

After the second full day of tests and procedures, Vern was still in critical condition. Doctors again expressed the likelihood that Vern would not survive the night. Infection was beginning to set in. The damaged soft tissue was inflamed. He was held together from hip to chest with staples and stitches. They believed that Vern would eventually succumb to his injuries.

Dorothy chose to hope. She prayed faithfully and earnestly that she would not become a widow. She stayed with him, watching him battle for his life amidst bandages, tubes, and life-monitoring machines.

Her faith paid off. Vern survived another night and another. After a week, however, Dorothy and her family were worried that Vern may survive but that his recovery would be limited. They feared he would live out the rest of his life in a nursing facility. He hadn't died, but had they lost him anyway? Had he survived only to be confined to a bed for the rest of his life? Depression and hopelessness were frequent. After he "awoke" from the medically induced coma, Vern became increasingly frustrated and despondent. He had survived, but he didn't seem to be recovering.

After two weeks in intensive care, Vern wasn't improving. The doctors puzzled over his case. It was astounding that he'd survived, but why wasn't his condition improving now? The numerous doctors who attended Vern disagreed on the best course of action. He was still plagued by infection since the oil and asphalt couldn't be completely removed from the internal organs and tissue. The deliberations had been ongoing, and no conclusion seemed to be acceptable to all parties.

Finally, one Saturday, Dorothy reported some good news to her husband—their ward was holding a fast for him. The next day, just about at the time the Wanship Ward was breaking their fast, doctors finally agreed to a plan of action. They would begin silver nitrate treatment. While it had been used successfully in the past, cutting edge antibiotics and other drugs had pushed silver nitrate treatments into an "unconventional treatment" category.

Only two days into the new treatment, it was obvious that Vern was responding well. After a few more days, he was transferred to a step-down unit, where he received more aggressive treatment for his orthopedic injuries.

Even then, doctors warned Dorothy and Vern not to expect too much. He would probably be confined to a wheelchair for the rest of his life. The accident had caused too much damage to his hip and legs to make a full recovery possible. Besides those injuries, he would still likely suffer the effects of the internal injuries. He would probably endure many more bouts of infection because of the burns and residual gravel and asphalt contamination. They wanted the couple to come to terms with a realistic prognosis.

Remembering the blessing he'd received when his son-in-law arrived at the hospital, Vern was determined to do all he could to recover. He knew that God would help him walk again. After a month of physical therapy and endless consultations with doctors, Vern was finally cleared to go home. Dorothy was thrilled to push Vern in his wheelchair through the hospital door.

Vern did walk again. Only one month after the accident, Vern was able to walk without assistance. Two months after the accident, he was back at work. He attributes his amazing survival and recovery to the blessings he received while in the hospital, especially that first one that Kurt voiced. He also credits members of his ward, who fasted that the doctors would know how to treat him.

Without the timely arrival of the paramedics and the medical helicopter, Vern would surely not have survived. Obviously, the Lord had been watching out for him, sending mortal angels to do their work and save his life.

Today, Vern is an octogenarian. He and Dorothy's six children have given them eighteen grandchildren and a handful of great-grandchildren. The damage to Vern's body left some lasting disabilities. He continues to walk with a limp, and his legs have a purplish-blue discoloration just beneath the skin's surface. Whenever he puts on his socks and shoes, he is reminded of the gift of life. He should have died, but he was given another opportunity—a blessing which he is grateful for.

COMMANDED BY PRIESTHOOD POWER

Theron Borup

Struggling to get to the surface, Theron Borup couldn't breathe. He was tangled in his parachute, and the weight of his life raft dragged him farther underwater. Flailing his arms, he tried to remain upright. In his panic, he accidently swallowed some seawater, and his throat constricted. Within seconds, everything went black.

***

After the Japanese attacked Pearl Harbor on December 7, 1941, Theron and his wife, Gladys, knew it was only a matter of time before they would be separated by the war. Since they had no children, Theron decided to enlist rather than wait to be drafted. He was a returned missionary, so he reasoned that he could encourage and support the many young LDS servicemen.

After completing basic training, Theron was assigned to a Consolidated B-24 Liberator, a heavy bomber. He was stationed on the small island of Namfoor, in the South Pacific, with the 307th Bomb Group, better known as the "Jungle Air Force Long Bombers." He served for nearly two years at Namfoor, earning more than enough combat points to go home, but he was also the leader of the small LDS branch at the base and felt a responsibility to continue to serve in that capacity.

As the leader of the branch, Theron watched membership grow to over forty people. They met each week to hold sacrament services and to teach one another from Church publications such as the *Improvement Era* and the *Instructor*. He was one of the oldest enlisted men, at thirty years old, and he was highly respected by the members for his faith and knowledge of gospel doctrine.

In September 1944, the order came down to organize a mission to attack the Japanese oil refinery in Borneo (on the east coast of today's

Malaysia). The target was heavily defended by hundreds of anti-aircraft weapons and a squadron of Japanese fighter aircraft. According to General Douglas MacAuthur, "It was the most strategically important Japanese target in the Pacific" because it was a primary source of aviation fuel for the Japanese.

It was to be the longest American bomb raid ever attempted. The entire distance was longer than flying from Los Angeles to New York. It would require sixteen hours, round trip. To allow for such a long flight, the planes had to be modified to carry more fuel. Three of the four bomb bays were adapted to hold large fuel tanks.

Rumors spread about the mission and its likelihood of success, but long before any official assignments were made, Theron felt that he would be assigned to this mission. The spiritual manifestation he received assured him that not only would he be appointed but that he would not lose his life at that time. This personal revelation was so strong that, days before he received the official notification, Theron wrote home to tell his wife that he would be assigned to this very dangerous mission and he would survive it.

All six bombers took off the night of September 29. Theron's plane was leading the contingent, and the crew settled in for the eight-hour flight. Tensions rose as they closed in on the target; each crew member took his position. Theron shifted his weight nervously as his eyes strained to spot the enemy fighters through the scattered clouds. He had to be ready at any moment to fire the .50 caliber M2 Browning machine gun at the incoming Japanese aircraft.

The pilot's voice called out to the crew through the interphone system, "The target has been sighted." They all knew what that meant: the pilot could not make any evasive maneuvers until the fifteen thousand pounds of explosives had safely cleared the aircraft.

Suddenly, out of the corner of his eye, Theron spied a swarm of Japanese fighters coming their way. Theron said a silent prayer, pleading for protection, as the shots began. The Americans directed a barrage of fire power in at the oncoming planes, and leading the formation, Theron's plane took the brunt of the enemy's retaliation. The rat-a-tat-tat of the bullets' impact filled the air. Theron and the other crew members bobbed up and down, firing their weapons.

The intensity continued for nearly five minutes until the pilot's voice was heard once again. "Bombs away." Suddenly, the planes banked sharply, starting back toward the safety of their home base. Their mission had been successful, their aim, near perfect, and black smoke billowed up from the refinery. The battle, though, was far from over.

Enemy fighters continued their unrelenting attack, and the Americans fought for their lives. "I got him," the tail gunman called out, and Theron looked to see black smoke engulfing one of the pursuing planes. The damaged aircraft peeled off and abandoned its attack. Finally, after several more tense minutes, the attack began to subside. The incoming fire began to wane as, one by one, the Japanese gave up their chase. The terror of the American crewmen slowly ebbed. They allowed themselves to hope that it was all over, that they'd make it home after all.

Suddenly, out of nowhere, a Japanese plane swooped behind Theron's plane, not twenty-five feet from the hull. An explosion rocked the plane as a .20 mm shell sent a flash of bright yellow flames into the cabin. Almost simultaneously, another shell struck the fuselage. And the aircraft was completely engulfed in another fireball.

The men worked furiously to extinguish the flames. Acrid, choking smoke filled the air, and once the fire was out, the crew was left to wonder how much damage had been done to the integrity of the plane. They didn't have to wonder long. Within seconds, the tail began to shake violently. With each passing moment, the vibrations grew more intense. The entire frame of the plane creaked and moaned, threatening to break apart.

Despite his best efforts, the pilot, Major Charles Pierce, could not hold the plane steady for much longer. He reluctantly gave the order through the interphone: "All crew stand by to bail out." The words sent a shock wave of fear through the men, but each prepared, collecting life jackets, parachutes, and life rafts as they awaited the signal to bail out.

Procedure called for the crewmen in the rear to be the first to bail after the alarm bell rang out. Major Pierce reported their current altitude—six thousand feet—and reminded the men to delay opening their chutes as long as possible to reduce their chance of being strafed by Japanese pilots.

The men waited, their patience wearing thin. Why hadn't the alarm been given? The plane continued to jerk violently, and the men feared it would soon break to pieces. Theron silently prayed that they would get out of the plane before that happened. They were headed straight down. If they didn't bail out soon, they may not get out in time to pull their chutes.

Finally, Staff Sergeant Bill Schmidtke negotiated the narrow catwalk to see why the alarm hadn't been sounded. He was shocked to find the cockpit empty. Screaming as loud as he could, he rushed back to the anxious men at the rear. "They're gone! Bail out! Bail out!"

The pilot had sounded the alarm precious minutes earlier, but for some reason, no one had heard it. Assuming the men in the rear had bailed out at the signal, Major Pierce and the four other men at the front of the plane had taken their turn to abandon the ruined aircraft.

The six remaining men saw the panic in Schmidtke's eyes as he hastily returned from the cockpit. "Bail out," he continued to shout. Each man found the closest exit, some climbing through the camera hatch and others using the rear bomb bay. Theron was the last to go, holding on as long as he dared before surrendering himself to the slipstream as he was jerked away from the plane. Suddenly, he was in a free fall, his arms and legs thrashing wildly as he fought the natural impulse to slow his descent by pulling the ripcord of his parachute.

Clenching the cord tightly, his hand quivered. He knew his life was in the balance—pull the cord too soon and become a target, pull it too late and he wouldn't survive the fall. He watched the approaching ocean carefully, and when he could see the white foam of the waves below, he yanked hard on the cord. The chute shot above him, rippling loudly in the wind until it burst open and filled with air. Dangling in the air, he drifted downward.

The danger from the Japanese was still real. When the four men at the front of the plane had bailed out, all but one had been hit and killed by enemy fire. For some reason, though, Theron didn't attract any gunfire.

As he neared the water, he gritted his teeth, bracing for impact. His boots hit first with a painful thud. Seconds later, the life-saving parachute turned deadly as it dragged him under the choppy water. Half conscious, he felt himself being towed downward. He thought of his wife and envisioned her weeping over his coffin. Suddenly, he came to his senses. "God save me," he pled silently.

With a sudden burst of strength, he somehow managed to escape the parachute rigging and swim to the surface, where he gulped in the delicious air. Knowing what he needed to do, he pulled out the life raft and the cartridge to inflate it. It wouldn't inflate.

He brought the raft to his mouth and attempted to inflate it manually. Even then, the raft would only partially inflate, but it was enough to keep him afloat. With all his remaining strength, Theron struggled up and into the half-inflated life raft, collapsing in exhaustion.

Theron rested for about thirty minutes, listening to the sound of the water lapping against the raft. When he began to survey his surroundings, he spotted a large ship moving toward him. He was thrilled to think that he'd be rescued so quickly until he realized that he was in enemy waters and the ship could very well be Japanese.

Nervously, Theron watched as the boat drew nearer to him. He thought of the rumors that the Japanese had been torturing American prisoners of war. He remembered the promise he'd been given that he'd survive, but for the first time he wondered if that meant becoming a prisoner of war. The closer it got, the more worried Theron became. His heart pounded as the flag came into focus—the Japanese flag, the rising red sun on a white background. He continued to watch as the ship approached, hoping against hope that he wouldn't be spotted.

Just as he had almost given up any possibility of avoiding capture, the ship made a sudden turn away from him. He held his breath as the ship's engines roared to life, and the boat picked up speed. Despite the bright yellow life raft, he had gone completely unnoticed by the ship's crew.

The following hours found Theron and some of his fellow crewmen tying their rafts together. The seven men floated aimlessly in enemy waters, discussing the fate of the men who had not survived the bail out. Theron realized that if the alarm had functioned properly, it was likely that none of them would have survived. He recognized this as yet another blessing from a loving Father in Heaven.

The surviving crew members elected Theron to manage their lone canteen of water and to protect the few remaining matches from those who would be tempted to smoke. Smoking may have brought temporary relief to their stress, but in the end it intensified their thirst.

The sun beat mercilessly down on the stranded men. It burned their skin and chapped their lips. By nightfall, their thirst seemed too much to bear and many looked longingly at the sea, tempted to sip just a little, but they helped each other. They supported and encouraged each other. Together they were able to resist the temptation.

The night went by without incident, but still their spirits sank. The hope of being rescued was becoming a distant one as the day passed by.

The next day was no better. A ferocious storm nearly tore the men from their life rafts. Expending their strength to stay afloat and to stay together, the men withstood the raging storm with swells as high as thirty feet. After the weather improved once more, the men discussed their fate.

They needed a plan. Most agreed they would rather be captured by the Japanese than stay stranded and die of thirst and exposure. They decided to head for the shore.

As they paddled, another storm approached. It blew them away from the land. They spotted a lighthouse and renewed their efforts, but it was no use. Their energy-sapped bodies were no match for the wind and waves. Discouraged, they finally abandoned their plan and stopped paddling. While the others were frustrated and disappointed, Theron again recognized the protective hand of God in their inability to reach the shore. With that knowledge, Theron prayed for comfort and soon felt a reassurance of peace.

By the third day, the men were lethargic. Their remaining strength was gone as was their hope of being rescued. Another powerful storm battered them further, and many lost the will to survive. They had endured three days with no food or water. Despondency and despair set in.

Just before the sun set that evening, someone noticed several small vessels a few miles away. A pillar of black smoke billowed skyward. But were those ships friend or foe? They hesitated to fire their only flare, fearing that it would lead to capture instead of rescue.

Without warning, a periscope emerged from the water a few hundred feet from the entourage. To their great joy, the men saw that it was an American submarine. As soon as they realized they were about to be rescued, they fired the flare. Their spirits soared as they anticipated the taste of purified water. However, minutes later their spirits plunged to further depths when the sub passed a mere two hundred feet from the conjoined rafts. Quietly, the submarine slipped under the water and disappeared once again, the crew completely unaware of the desperate plight of their comrades.

Again, the men gave up hope. They thought they had once again expended the last of their energy anticipating their imminent rescue. They were thrust into a state of deepest hopelessness—all except Theron. Though his faith was being tried, Theron was determined to cling to the confirmation he had received that he would survive the mission.

The bright yellowish moon illuminated the shimmering ocean, and frustration grew to anger, as many of the men complained openly against God for not saving them. Theron wouldn't stand for it, and he warned them about being ungrateful that God had spared their lives thus far. He reminded them that despite the Japanese planes constantly flying overhead, their bright yellow rafts were never spotted. Despite Theron's reminder, stomachs growled, and men longed for a quick death rather than a prolonged starvation.

Accepting that they were destined to die, the men spoke candidly to one another about what came next, after this life. At one point one of the men asked Theron how he stayed so positive in light of the dire circumstances. Instantly, they all seemed curious to hear Theron's thoughts about why God hadn't saved them.

Theron bore a powerful testimony and revealed his conviction that they would yet be rescued. He feared they wouldn't understand if he told them how he knew, but he firmly reiterated, "I know in my heart we'll be rescued." His unwavering confidence sustained the men for a little while longer. They wanted to believe him, but it was not easy.

The morning of the fourth day dawned, and the heat once more grew oppressive. Unexpectedly, a submarine tower once more breached the surface. Knowing this was probably their last chance to be rescued, the men gathered what little strength remained and waved. They made as much noise as they could, but once again their hopes were dashed as the sub turned away and continued on. The cheering stopped.

As he watched that latest hope pick up speed, leaving the men once more in its wake, Theron received a prompting, "You have the priesthood. Command that submarine to return and pick you up."

Theron obediently bowed his head and softly uttered the words. "In the name of Jesus Christ and by the power of the holy Melchizedek Priesthood, I command that submarine to turn around and pick us up." As he ended the spoken prayer, he continued to pray in his heart. He watched hopefully, fully expecting the sub to turn around. Seconds passed. "Turn around. Come on, turn around."

His eyes were glued to the scene, and suddenly he realized that the sub was making a wide turn back in their direction. The submarine slowly continued to turn until it was pointed at the floating life rafts. The men were afraid to hope, remembering the disappointment of the many opportunities that had passed them by.

Grown men wept unashamedly as they were hauled on board the USS *Mingo*. The three-hundred-foot sub had stopped just a few feet from them, and the seamen reached out to help the soldiers aboard.

Inside, the captain invited Theron to his cabin, where he tried to explain what had happened. "I don't know how we ever found you. We weren't even looking for you." He went on to say that for some unexplained reason he'd felt compelled to change direction. When they did, the life rafts were spotted by an attentive naval officer.

Theron knew exactly why they had been rescued. He offered a quick, silent prayer of thanks not only that his life was spared but for the constant reassurance that he was always under God's watchful care.

LION ATTACK

Paul Oakey

PAUL OAKEY HAD BEEN IN Guatemala for almost twenty months and was just a few months from completing his LDS mission there. Paul was a zone leader responsible for sixteen other missionaries, including three sisters. The missionaries had decided to spend their preparation day together doing some sightseeing in Esquipulas, one of the most isolated towns in Guatemala, only miles from the Honduran border.

It had been a fun morning. The group had seen several sights in town and still had some time left over. Local Church members had recommended visiting the nearby zoo, The Ecological Park Cueva de las Minas. It was nestled in a mountainside valley outside of town. The park boasted twenty-five species of animals.

The missionaries laughed and joked along the way, enjoying the beauty of the countryside and one another's company. After about an hour-long hike, they reached the zoo. Paying the small admission fee, the companions walked the dirt paths leading to each exhibit.

Some were a little unnerved by the conditions of the park. It was unlike any zoo they had visited in the United States. The quality and safety of the animal enclosures seemed a little questionable. But no one around them seemed to mind as they meandered through the jungle setting of the park, so the group set aside those feelings of caution and followed the crowd.

Most of the exhibits were set off by cages. There were no buffer zones to keep curious spectators from getting too close to the bars. At the monkey cage, some of the missionaries began feeding the primates with animal food they had purchased at the zoo. Everyone was amused at the tactics of the seemingly tame creatures until one of the monkeys stole the camera of an unwary missionary. The others roared with laughter as the missionary looked on helplessly while the monkey scampered away, camera in hand.

Finally, they arrived at the most popular attraction—the pair of African lions. Visitors looked on with an uncomfortable vulnerability. Like the other cages, this one seemed inadequate to contain the wild beasts. The bars were a mere half-inch in diameter and so far apart that a child could easily step inside. The cage seemed a little small for the two adult lions lounging within.

As the missionaries approached, they were impressed at the size of the lions. The creatures looked a little emaciated, but they still appeared majestic, resting quietly in the tropical heat. One of the lions was slightly larger than the other, but both were obviously powerful creatures.

Talking and laughing, the missionaries gathered together for a group photo. As they posed, Paul began to survey the surroundings, looking for a more interesting angle. Paul's father, a professional photographer, had taught Paul how to make a snapshot more interesting. Paul looked for a distinctive angle to improve his picture. Finally, he spotted the perfect setup—a ten-foot ledge at the rear of the lions' enclosure.

Following the worn path away from the front of the cage, Paul made his way to the ledge. With little effort he pulled himself up. From his new vantage point, he quickly glanced toward the lions, finding that this really would be a perfect shot.

He pulled out his camera and began to adjust the settings when, suddenly, out of the corner of his eye, he saw a flash of movement. The larger of the lions leapt toward Paul, its massive paw approaching almost without warning. It reached through the gap in the bars and latched onto Paul's calf. He screamed as the sharp claws dug deep in his flesh.

The 400-pound animal easily overpowered its prey. It yanked feverishly at Paul's leg, trying to pull him completely inside the cage. Paul fought with all his might to keep himself wedged against the bars. He knew that if the lion succeeded in getting him into the enclosure, it would be an almost-certain death sentence. Paul flailed his arms, striking the lion repeatedly with his fist, but the creature didn't even react.

The frenzy of flying dirt caught the attention of some of the missionaries. A few even laughed, thinking Paul was joking. Suddenly, Paul snapped. His adrenaline was pumping wildly; his fear and anger got the better of him. He swore loudly enough for the other missionaries to hear. "This lion has my leg!"

Paul's language caught their attention. They knew something must be seriously wrong. Every missionary's head snapped to watch Paul battle with the ferocious beast. As they watched, horrified, the second lion joined in the struggle. It clamped ahold of his left arm, pulling it completely inside the bars.

Paul was pinned several feet above the ground. His chest and face pressed painfully against the metal bars, and his leg and arm were in the unyielding grasp of the frenzied animals. Stunned, the other missionaries rushed to Paul's aid, but they weren't sure what to do. If they simply jumped in, they too could be caught in the fray.

Elder Lopez scanned the ground, searching for anything he could use as a weapon. Elder Anderson went to Paul. He stood directly beneath the screaming young man, supporting him so that if the lions did release their grip, Paul wouldn't fall backwards.

The lions continued yanking and twisting, doing everything they could to get Paul fully in their grasp. Paul hadn't quit his assault either. Finding his blows to the lion's head useless, Paul tried a different tactic. He pushed his thumb into the beast's eye. He'd hoped the pain would cause it to free him, but the lion barely winced at Paul's feeble attempt to hurt it.

Paul had been desperately resisting for almost two minutes, and his strength was quickly fading. His arm and leg were bleeding profusely, and the pain was intensifying. Just then, Elder Lopez joined the struggle with a large pole. He aimed for the smaller lion's mouth, hoping to pry its jaws open and free Paul's arm.

Finally, two security workers came running to investigate the ruckus. Seeing their rifles, Paul shouted, "Shoot them!" But instead the workers pointed the guns skyward and fired. They hoped to scare the lions without actually injuring them. The lions were undeterred.

The sisters couldn't bear to watch, and not knowing what else to do, they knelt together in prayer. Paul kept at the lion's eye, and Elder Lopez thrust the pole at it with all his strength. Just as the sisters finished their prayer, the smaller lion released Paul's arm.

With that pressure gone, Paul fell backward a bit, but the larger animal still clung to his calf. Elder Anderson supported his friend's weight as best he could, and the repositioning allowed Paul to kick at the lion with his other foot. Attempting to readjust its grasp, the lion briefly let go, but that was all it took.

Paul hit the ground with a thud, landing in a pool of blood. Immediately, he began writhing in pain. The missionaries sprang into action, trying to be as gentle as possible as they moved Paul away from the enclosure. Elder Anderson, who had been beneath Paul, was covered in the injured elder's blood, but he ignored it all, lifting Paul's head and offering him a drink of water. Paul sipped slowly, but he coughed as he tried to swallow.

Elder Lopez immediately pulled out his vial of consecrated oil and asked Elder Anderson to assist him in giving Paul a blessing. After the anointing, Elder Lopez commanded Paul to live then offered additional blessings of peace and comfort.

Seeing the panic in his friends' eyes, Paul tried to reassure them. He asked them to get his camera and start taking pictures, saying, "This doesn't happen every day." Some chuckled nervously, but they knew his life was in jeopardy, and they waited anxiously for help.

Someone had called an ambulance, and zoo personal hurried to the scene carrying bandages and other first aid items. They wrapped his wounds tightly, but they couldn't stop the steady flow of blood. As each minute passed, Paul grew more and more dizzy and weak. The blood dripped through the soaked bandages.

Another twenty minutes passed before the crowd heard the sirens in the distance. The sound grew closer until the "ambulance" drove into the park. It was nothing more than a stripped-down minivan. There was no real medical equipment inside, just the driver and an assistant. The two quickly jumped out of the vehicle and pulled a stretcher from the back. Knowing how critical each minute was, two missionaries carried Paul to the ambulance and gently lifted him onto the vinyl-covered stretcher.

The ride in the back of the ambulance was agonizing. As much as possible, the driver avoided sharp turns and bumps in the roads. Elder Lopez and Elder Anderson had climbed into the van with Paul and tried to comfort him as they sped toward the nearest medical facilities.

Paul asked Elder Lopez to check for cell phone service and alert him when they could use the phone. Within minutes, Elder Lopez was dialing the number Paul recited. Handing the phone to Paul, Elder Lopez told him, "I think it's ringing."

"Dad?" Paul's voice quivered as he spoke.

"Paul?" His father answered, confused. "What's going on?" Alan Oakey didn't know why his son was unexpectedly calling home. He knew something must be wrong.

"Dad, I can't talk long," Paul struggled to form the words. "I'm going to the hospital right now because I was attacked by a lion at a zoo we were visiting. I'll be all right," he continued. "I just wanted to let you know so you weren't surprised."

Surprised? Paul's father was stunned. Instantly, hundreds of questions ran through his mind until one finally popped out: "A lion? What kind of lion?"

"It was one of the big cats, Dad. You know, the ones with manes?"

"Oh." Alan was still trying to process the information. "How bad are you hurt?"

Not wanting to worry his father, Paul downplayed the incident. He didn't mention the amount of blood he'd lost nor the throbbing pain in his arm and leg. "I'll be okay." He tried to sound convincing. "I'm losing my cell service. I'll call you later and let you know what they say, okay? Gotta go. Bye."

Paul's head spun. He tried to hand the phone back to his companion. Looking down, Paul noticed the blood pooling on the floor of the ambulance. He was quickly losing consciousness. At last they pulled into a local clinic, but everything went black. Before he even entered the doors, Paul had lost consciousness.

***

Health care is limited for the outlying communities in Guatemala. Residents are forced to rely on doctors who travel from town to town. The people rarely know when they will be able to see a doctor. These physicians have varying degrees of training, and most serious cases are referred to the larger hospitals in the cities, but in emergencies, critically injured patients often die in transit.

This likely would have been the case with Paul if there hadn't been an American-trained physician visiting Esquipulas that afternoon. The physician had been trained in vascular surgery and wasn't even supposed to be there that day. But his expertise was put to good use.

By the time Paul arrived at the clinic, he had lost approximately sixty percent of his blood. An artery in his arm had been badly damaged, and several veins had been severed. He was fading in and out of consciousness, and it was clear that if they didn't stop the bleeding, Paul would die. The doctor immediately ordered that the staff prepare the young man for surgery.

Despite an ill-supplied operating room, the surgeon was able to clamp the damaged artery and stop the bleeding. He was also able to locate both ends of the severed veins and surgically splice them together. All this was accomplished without the benefit of a surgical microscope, which is typically necessary for such detailed and precision surgery.

Now that the blood flow had been stopped, they needed to deal with replenishing the nearly seven pints that Paul had already lost. His blood pressure was critically low, and it was crucial that he receive a transfusion immediately.

Unfortunately, the underdeveloped medical facilities offered little by way of blood. Luckily, the other missionaries had arrived at the clinic, willing to donate. Transfusing Paul with the wrong blood type could be fatal, but the missionaries all carried a card listing their blood type, so precious minutes were saved since they could bypass the testing.

To save time, the doctor ordered a direct transfusion. As Paul laid unconscious, one-by-one the missionaries lined up to have their blood flow directly into Paul's arm. Nine of the seventeen missionaries were able to donate, and within an hour, Paul had received enough blood to be out of immediate danger.

***

Dr. Craig MacArthur, the Church's physician for the Guatemala South mission was in Guatemala City when he heard the news about Paul. The driving conditions were too dangerous at night, so Dr. MacArthur had to wait until the next day to depart. He arrived in Esquipulas the next afternoon, where he found Paul still unconscious and barely responsive.

Dr. MacArthur notified the hospital that he would be moving Paul to Guatemala City, a four-hour drive from the clinic. Paul couldn't be moved until he was stable, though. At first it didn't seem possible that he would be able to make the trip, but by 2:30 that afternoon, Paul was headed to the capital city in an ambulance.

Paul was unconscious for most of that trip. He was no longer losing large amounts of blood, but he remained in critical condition. It had been over forty-eight hours since the attack, and the wounds were becoming infected.

Swelling was a major concern. Shortly after they left Esquipulas, Paul's arm ballooned to nearly three times its normal size. When they arrived at the larger hospital in Guatemala City, doctors rushed Paul into surgery. They performed an emergency fasciotomy to relieve the tension and prevent further tissue damage caused by swelling.

The following morning, Paul's arm was still swollen, and the infection was taking over his whole body; E. coli and other unknown bacteria from the lions' mouths and claws had infected the missionary's wounds.

Dr. MacArthur realized the advanced antibiotics available in the United States were Paul's only hope of surviving the raging infections. He needed to get Paul to a hospital where he could receive those treatments.

He called Church headquarters to arrange for a medical evacuation to Utah, but they informed him the jet could not depart from the United States until Paul was medically cleared to travel. Luckily, that didn't take too long, and twenty-four hours later, Dr. MacArthur boarded the plane with Paul. Less than five hours later, they were in Salt Lake City.

Paul slept through the plane ride and through the ambulance ride to the hospital, but as he entered the emergency room doors, the pain killers were beginning to wear off. He was in agony. The pain didn't subside, and night after night, Paul cried silently in his bed, praying for deliverance and help in dealing with the unbearable pain. Though doctors tried to relieve his suffering, no pain medication offered relief.

Paul awoke Sunday morning, nearly a week after the attack, still in a considerable amount of pain. His spirits were boosted by a visit from Elder Richard G. Hinckley, who was responsible for overseeing the missionary department. Elder Hinckley gave Paul a blessing and told Paul that the Quorum of the Twelve had convened in the temple to pray specifically for the young man. This offered some comfort to Paul and his family.

But later that afternoon, Paul was once again feeling discouraged. His arms and legs were wrapped in bandages, and he was frustrated that nothing could be done to alleviate his pain. That was when he received another visitor. A man pushing a wheelchair entered the room. In the wheelchair sat Elder Boyd K. Packer.

After a short visit, Elder Packer was preparing to leave when Paul stopped him. "Can I ask you a favor?"

"Why certainly," Elder Packer replied, eager to do what he could to help the suffering patient.

"Could you touch me . . . just so I know this is real?" Paul had been under the confusing influence of pain medication, so he wanted to make sure that this was not just another dream.

"I certainly can, young man." Elder Packer reached up and gently rested his hand on Paul's upper right arm, the only place not covered with bandages.

Later that evening as Paul reflected on the uplifting visits he'd had that day, he was again surprised when Elder Russell M. Nelson entered his room.

They chatted for a moment, but before leaving, Elder Nelson asked Paul if he'd like a blessing. Paul readily agreed. Among the promises he received, Paul was especially touched by the words, "As an Apostle of the Lord Jesus Christ and by that authority, I bless you to be healed."

For the first time since the attack, Paul felt at peace. He was hopeful that everything would turn out. He knew the Lord loved him.

After numerous surgeries and over a month-long stay in the hospital, Paul was finally discharged. Doctors made every attempt to save Paul's left arm, but it would never be the same again. Paul had a choice of keeping the useless arm in a sling or having it amputated and being fitted with a prosthetic. Hoping to retain some use, he chose to get a prosthetic, and in September, two months after the incident, doctors amputated his arm just below the elbow.

As Paul reflects on this unpleasant incident, he points to a scar in the palm of his right hand. It remains one of the most powerful reminders of how God spared his life. He has no recollection of being bitten or cut on his hand. However, he's grateful for this unique scar. It reminds him of the marks on the Savior's hands and that God protected him and allowed him to survive this most incredible, life-changing experience.

STROKE OF LUCK

SARAH FREDERICKSON

TUESDAY MORNING, SEPTEMBER 6, 2011, began like most other days for Sarah Frederickson. She was working at her desk. At 10:00 a.m., she took a phone call then wrenched her neck both ways to "pop" it. She was immediately overcome with dizziness. It became so intense she thought she would pass out. Overwhelmed with vertigo, she immediately called a coworker to come to her desk and cover for her. He took one look at her and said, "Do you want me to call 911?"

Sarah brushed off the suggestion, then slumped to the floor with her head between her knees, trying to get rid of the dizziness. Another coworker heard about the commotion and came to escort Sarah to the restroom, where she collapsed to the floor and began to vomit violently.

Julie, the office manager, was concerned. She escorted Sarah to an empty office to lie down. She offered Sarah a blanket and a cool cloth for her forehead. Sarah writhed in misery. She thought perhaps she had food poisoning, but her condition continued to worsen.

Julie called Sarah's sister and roommate, Rachel. She suggested that Rachel come pick Sarah up and bring her to the emergency room. Rachel immediately set out but was delayed.

Luckily, Sarah felt a distinct impression not to wait for her sister. She asked Julie to call 911. The time seemed to drag by, and Sarah seemed to be in a lot of pain. Her coworkers tried to make her comfortable as they silently urged the ambulance to arrive.

Finally, the EMTs rushed through the door into the office where Sarah lay. They scrambled about, trying to determine the cause of Sarah's symptoms. They checked vitals, stabilized their patient, then tried to decide what to do next.

They hadn't seen any sign of serious problems, so one emergency responder attempted to dissuade Sarah from going to the hospital. Sarah wasn't listening to his reasons. She knew something was wrong. She knew she needed to get to the hospital.

At Sarah's insistence, the EMTs wheeled her to the back of the ambulance and loaded her on board. They transported her to Inova Fairfax Hospital.

The ambulance ride was terrifying. Sarah couldn't stop vomiting copious amounts of coffee-colored granules of blood into towel after towel after towel. In the emergency room, it took four different nurses to finally get an IV into her arm.

By this time, Rachel had finally arrived. She lovingly helped Sarah into the hospital gown. Sarah was shaken by the look on her sister's face. She could see the fear in Rachel's eyes. Rachel thought she was going to die. Sarah drifted in and out of consciousness for the next seven hours as her sister faithfully kept vigil.

After arriving at the hospital, Rachel knew the seriousness of her sister's condition and immediately called her cousins, Sam and Andrew, to give Sarah a priesthood blessing. Sarah was unconscious, but Rachel drew strength from the words. The blessing counseled Sarah to listen to and obey the doctors and to be patient with the process. If she did those things, she would return to full health and strength.

Rachel watched her sister carefully. Sarah lay in a fetal position, curled in a ball, eyes shut. She looked small and almost lifeless. If she moved, she threw up. Rachel answered questions about her sister and observed as doctors ordered test after test—no closer to diagnosing the quickly deteriorating patient. They drew blood and did a CAT scan, a lower intestinal workup, and several other internal tests. The bloody coughing was a sign of internal bleeding, but the doctors just couldn't find where it was coming from.

Sarah continued to vomit blood. Nearly eight hours after Sarah was admitted, the doctor was at her wit's end. Needing answers from the unconscious patient, the doctor jarred Sarah awake.

"I need you to concentrate," she told the weakened girl. "Have you been in a car accident?"

"No," Sarah answered.

"Have you hit your head or had any sort of head injury?"

"No."

The doctor was growing frustrated. "Have you had any recent neck injuries?"

In her groggy, debilitated state, somehow it clicked. "I popped my neck right before I started to get dizzy."

The doctor immediately ordered an MRI then explained to Rachel, "I think your sister had a stroke."

***

The secret to successful stroke treatment lies in rapid diagnosis. The longer the treatment is delayed, the more potential there is for lasting consequences. The ideal time frame for treating a stroke is two hours. After that, the most common outcome is brain damage. This damage causes severe physical defects that affect talking and swallowing or cause paralysis and memory loss. It can also affect cognitive functions, and in extreme cases, the patient can be left brain dead. Sarah's stroke had not been diagnosed for nearly eight hours.

Fortunately, when the EMTs had determined which hospital to take Sarah to, they chose Inova Fairfax Hospital—a certified Primary Stroke Center. Had she waited for Rachel to drive her to the hospital, they likely would have gone to Virginia Hospital Center because it was closer to their home. It was another evidence that someone was watching over Sarah.

***

Sarah and her sister Rachel shared a condo in Washington, D.C. The rest of their family was miles away, so while she waited, Rachel was making phone calls to her mother in Utah. Helpless to physically assist from such a distance, the girls' mother prayed and sent out text messages and e-mails to friends and family asking for their prayers, then she began making arrangements to catch the red-eye to D.C.

Finally, the MRI results were in, and the doctor explained that, apparently, when Sarah had popped her neck, she'd somehow dissected the left vertebral artery, causing it to bleed. It had been bleeding continuously for the last eight hours. Sarah was rushed into the Neuroscience Intensive Care Unit (NICU).

Rachel had informed their bishop, and he was on the way with his counselors. They visited, asked what they could do, and gave her a blessing of comfort. Their blessing reiterated the promise of full recovery if she followed her doctors' counsel.

In the meantime, Sarah had become something of a celebrity in the hospital. The doctors believed it was a miracle that she was still living. Rachel was frequently giving doctors updates on her sister's condition. The neurologist explained that she was the first patient he'd ever seen with no serious side effects from a major stroke. He could not explain it. For days, Sarah was the talk of the hospital.

Though the news was encouraging, Sarah's ordeal was not over. She tossed and turned through the night and the following day. The pain increased. Both her neck and the base of her skull throbbed, keeping Sarah from getting the rest she needed. Her requests for pain medication began to occur more frequently. She went from one dose every six hours, to one every four hours, to one every two hours. By the next evening she was in excruciating pain, but when she was asked to rate her level of pain, she invariably told them it was a four or five out of ten. As an athlete she'd played through many injuries. She had a high tolerance for pain, and she admitted, she "didn't want to look like a wimp."

Not knowing the extent of Sarah's pain, the nurse told her that she was to be released to a step-down care unit until they performed a routine CAT scan scheduled for early the next morning. That plan didn't bother Sarah, but Rachel was concerned because of the amount of pain her sister was in. After the CAT scan, Sarah persuaded Rachel to go home and get some things. Though Rachel was hesitant to leave, Sarah assured her everything would be okay.

Sarah was barely settled into the step down unit when four nurses came rushing into her room. They had been instructed to get her back to the NICU. Her doctor had been shocked when he looked at the results of her CAT scan. It revealed that her brain was still swelling, and there was an imminent danger of the blood supply being cut off to vital parts of her brain.

After another surgery, Sarah spent five more days in the NICU. Her speech and ability to text were never impaired. For the first few days, she had some minor balance issues and nausea. She was, at times, slightly confused, and it took her a little longer than normal to answer a question. She wasn't really great at the "touch your nose, touch my finger" drill with her left hand. But her condition was truly remarkable.

Also remarkable was the surge of support. Sarah's coworkers, friends, extended family, and members of her ward, even some who didn't personally know her, rallied to her side with offers of financial assistance, expressions of love, visits, blessings, prayers, and bedside watches when she was awake and while she slept. They brought cards, gifts, balloons, flowers, books, magazines, and food galore to the hospital and to her apartment when she returned. Friends in Utah watched over the remaining family members there and sent up prayers on behalf of those across the country. Phone calls, messages of concern, love, and support for Sarah were sent via e-mail and posted to Facebook by friends around the world.

When the news came that she'd be transferred to the stroke step down unit, she and Rachel threw a pizza party for the nurses and staff that had done so much for the sisters.

According to her doctors, Sarah is a "walking miracle." They still cannot explain how someone who suffered a major stroke in the cerebellum region—the region of the brain associated with motor control—could experience so few lasting effects. Today, she is back to her normal routine: walking, coaching a girls' basketball team, and playing basketball, coed football, and coed softball. She is still a star player.

Sarah and her family are grateful for the many people in today's world who know, understand, and practice charity; who access the power that comes through prayer; who trust and wait upon God; and who see and experience his power in their lives.

"MAY GOD GRANT THAT HE MAY SURVIVE" (MORMON 1:2)

Dan Liljenquist

I'm going to die!

He'd always known that he would die one day, but Dan Liljenquist had no idea that he would be facing death so soon.

It had been an unremarkable Sunday morning: the group of volunteers had boarded the small Cessna at the international airport in Guatemala. They were headed for the small village of El Estor on a humanitarian project to build an addition to the schoolhouse there.

Dan—president of Focus Services, a large Utah-based telemarketing company—was accompanied by four of his employees. John Carter, Cody Odekirk, Jeff Reppe, and Lydia Silva had each written an essay about why they wanted to be a part of this week-long excursion. They had been picked as winners and now followed Dan and the other volunteers onto the plane.

Assuming others would want to sit up front to see the action in the cockpit, Dan graciously moved to the seat in the back. He just wanted a quiet, well-lit seat so he could read for the ninety-minute flight. The atmosphere buzzed with excitement as the rest of the passengers found their seats and awaited takeoff.

Everything seemed to be going smoothly until about halfway into the flight. The plane's engine had made a horrible noise and ground to a halt. For a moment all was quiet, then Dan heard the panic in the voices of the pilots. They couldn't restart the engine.

Monica Bonilla and her copilot, Fernando Estrada, tried to maintain as much altitude as possible, postponing the inevitable crash landing, but slowly the plane drew nearer and nearer to the jungle below. Bonilla sent out a distress call and instructed the passengers to make sure they were tightly buckled in. Thick, black smoke billowing from the right side of the plane wafted inside the cabin, and everyone realized the gravity of their situation.

Dan looked around, wondering if the others were also preparing themselves to die. He was at peace. He thought of his temple covenants, reviewing the temple recommend questions in his mind. While he knew he'd be okay, his chest constricted when he thought about his family—his wife, each of his children. He pictured them one by one, mentally offering each a farewell. Finally, he turned to John. "If it's our time, it's our time."

John stared out the window, apparently deep in thought about his family. He turned to Dan, nodding his head. "If it's our time, it's our time."

After four minutes of somber silence, they glided closer to the trees. Without warning the plane banked sharply to the right. The pilots had seen an open space in the distance and diligently worked to clear the remaining trees to land in the field. A collective gasp echoed through the cabin and someone screamed as the plane continued to bank hard, narrowly missing the mountains.

As the plane neared the ground, Dan focused on the moment. His heart pounded furiously. There was no escape. No alternative but to simply hunker down and hope—until the thought came into his mind to pray. "Heavenly Father, I feel like there is more for me to do. But thy will be done," he whispered to himself.

Suddenly, Dan thought to lie down in the back of the plane. There wasn't really any room, but Dan tried to improvise. Still in his seat belt, he slid toward the floor and grabbed the handhold on the door, preparing for impact.

Impact was just seconds away. Just as Dan lifted his head to peek out the window of the cockpit, an eruption of sound and light blasted through the cabin. The plane instantly broke into pieces: The left wing was ripped from the fuselage. The roof instantly smashed into the passenger seats. Pieces of airplane debris showered the cabin like tiny missiles. The fuel tanks ruptured on impact, sending waves of combustible liquid in all directions.

Dan was hit on the head and blacked out. When he regained consciousness, he was in a fog of confusion. As he looked down at his legs, it was obvious something was wrong, but in his state of shock, he wasn't exactly sure what. He unbuckled his seat belt and fell forward. As he reached out to catch himself, he was startled by the sight of his arms in the sunlight. "I'm alive. I'm alive," he repeated aloud.

Still dazed, he tried to stand, but he couldn't. He looked down at his legs. His left foot was twisted, seeming broken at the ankle. His right leg was also broken, his knee pointed one direction and his foot pointed the opposite way. Strangely, he couldn't sense much pain.

As his mind began to clear, he started looking around, taking in his surroundings and searching for other survivors. Ten of the fourteen passengers, however, had been killed instantly when the plane hit the ground. He did hear someone moaning. It was April Jensen. She was still strapped in her seat, but she was horribly burned. Dan could barely make out her words: "The plane's on fire."

Looking for an escape route, Dan could see a small flicker of flames through the gaps between the seats. Suddenly, the fuel ignited, and the flames exploded into the woman's face. Dan's pant legs caught fire, as did much of the debris strewn throughout what remained of the cabin.

His broken legs were temporarily forgotten in the urgency Dan felt to flee from the encroaching fire. He tried once more to stand. Finding that impossible, Dan rolled onto his back and used his hands to pull his injured legs from beneath the wreckage. He began to drag himself toward the door, negotiating not only the scattered debris but also the bodies of his friends. His legs dangled uselessly behind him, and he repeated to himself, "Not today . . . Today is not my day . . . Today is *not* my day."

Inch by agonizing inch, he moved slowly to the door. Just as he reached the exit, he looked up to see two men standing over him. They both appeared to be Guatemalan, one about sixty and the other only slightly younger. They each grabbed one of Dan's arms and hastily pulled him away from the remains of the aircraft. They dragged him across a grassy field, finally extinguishing the flames on his pants.

When they were satisfied with the distance, the two men eased Dan to the ground and rushed back to the plane. April Jensen couldn't unbuckle her seat belt and was calling out for help. Her clothing had caught fire, but unfazed, the two men worked bravely to free her from the blaze. Her nineteen-year-old daughter, Sarah, had also survived, miraculously with only bruises and cuts. April's husband and son, however, had not survived.

The men also returned to rescue Liz Johnson from the crash. She had been badly burned and was still fully engulfed in flames. After lifting her out of her seat and through the door, the men tried everything to extinguish the flames consuming her clothing. They finally resorted to throwing loose soil over her, which finally put the flames out. Sadly, Liz would die early the next morning in the hospital.

Dan watched the rescue efforts from thirty feet. He was horrified at what he saw: Inside the broken plane he could still see many of his friends buckled into their seats as the flames intensified. He searched for any signs of life but finally had to turn away from the horrific scene as an overwhelming feeling of despair overcame him. They were all dead, and there was nothing he could do to save them.

Then, as the adrenaline began to fade, Dan felt excruciating pain in his legs. Trying to distract himself, Dan reached into his pocket for his cell phone. He scanned through the photos, looking especially for pictures of his children. *It's just pain*, he told himself. *You'll get to see your family again.* He longed to speak to his wife, to hear her comforting voice.

These thoughts were interrupted by the boom of a sudden explosion. The heat was intense, and within seconds the flames were racing toward him, feeding on the fuel that had leaked as the plane descended and crash landed. He looked frantically for a safe haven he could crawl to, but it was no use. The flames were coming too fast, and he had no strength left to drag himself away from the danger.

Dan didn't realize, however, that at that moment two teenage boys were rushing to his aid. They carefully grasped Dan under his arms and dragged him out of sight of the plane, resting him near a small dirt road.

As he lay in the irrigation ditch, Dan heard another powerful explosion; this one rocked the countryside. He thought of his friends. He thought of how he would never see them again, about how he had been the one to survive, about all he would do with this second chance. Curious onlookers milled about, stunned by the events of the last few minutes. The people, wanting to help, delivered bottles of dirty water and insisted that he drink. Dan watched as ants crawled all over his body. It all seemed so surreal.

An ambulance arrived, and workers carefully helped Dan onto a stretcher. After he was secured, the vehicle sped away, leaving behind the chaos and the remains of the ill-fated Cessna.

The ambulance ride was incredibly painful for Dan. The nearest hospital was nearly forty-five minutes away on dirt roads. Each bump caused him terrible pain. He felt the grinding of his bones as they hit each dip and pothole.

The paramedic noticed the tears flowing from the corner of Dan's eyes. With great tenderness, she took his hand and lovingly held it throughout the trip. This simple yet incredible act of kindness brought her patient great comfort.

When they arrived at the hospital in Cuapas, Dan waited to be treated by the doctor. A kind nurse, seeming to read his mind, offered, "Would you like to call your family?" Dan readily accepted.

His heart sank, however, when the answering machine picked up. He realized his wife must be in church, so he just left a message: "Brooke, we've been in a plane accident. Everyone's dead. I'm going to be okay, but John's dead, Cody's dead, Jeff's dead, Lydia's dead." He paused. Just saying it all made the sting of their death real and painful. "They're taking me into surgery. I'll call you as soon as I can. I love you. Bye."

After a surgery to temporarily stabilize his legs, Dan was awoken and told he would be transferred with the two badly burned women to Guatemala City. Aside from the anesthesia during surgery, Dan had yet to receive any pain medications. He suffered even more while the helicopter jerked and bounced. One of the helicopter's crew members noticed Dan's discomfort, and he moved to sit next to Dan. Without saying a thing, he gently ran his fingers through Dan's hair. The simple, comforting gesture distracted Dan from the pain.

When they arrived at the hospital in Guatemala City, Dan was rushed to get X-rays taken. His clothing was cut away. Zuela, one of the nurses, took note of Dan's clothes and realized that he was LDS. "Can I get the elders for you?" she asked.

"Yes!" Dan replied through the excruciating pain.

The Guatemala City temple was a mere three hundred yards from the hospital, so that's where Zuela went. She convinced two elderly gentlemen there to return to the hospital with her. The dialect the men spoke was one that Dan could not comprehend, but though the words may not have been completely understood, the message was sweet and powerful.

A hospital worker offered Dan a cell phone so he could call home, but still, no one answered. Finally, he tried to call his wife's cell. He was relieved when she answered. "Brooke," he began, "we've been in a plane crash."

"That's not funny," she warned.

Dan closed his eyes. "No, it's true. They're all dead."

There was silence on the line. Finally, Brooke asked, "How are you?"

"Well," Dan wanted to downplay the seriousness of his condition, not wanting to worry her, "both my legs are broken, and I've got some burns. But I'll be alright." They talked for a few minutes. Dan told her more of the details but soon had to end the call. "I'm glad I could tell you before you heard about it somewhere else. I love you, and please tell the kids I love them too."

That night, doctors in Guatemala City performed surgery on Dan's legs. His right ankle was broken in sixteen places and had to be held together with numerous screws. His left leg required the insertion of a titanium rod.

Two days later Dan's father and brother—both physicians—arrived in Guatemala City to provide any necessary medical assistance. Two days after their arrival, Dan was stable enough to fly back to the United States. Though he flew first class, the pain was still unbearable. Despite the pain, the trip was worth it when Dan saw his family. His eight-year-old son came out to the car to greet Dan as soon as he pulled into the driveway. Dan began sobbing—tears of joy and relief.

For five weeks, Dan had to use a wheelchair and continues to walk with a limp, enduring continuous pain. Looking back, he still struggles with the seeming randomness of his survival, but he recognizes that he learned a great deal. He recounts three lessons in particular. First, the covenants we make bring us blessings of peace. These covenants can bring us comfort in times of need. Second, family is what matters the most. And finally, the memory of Christlike service never fades. He cherishes the memories of the kindness he was shown throughout the ordeal.

"I've always known conceptually that I was going to die, but after this, it became a reality. Because of that insight, I feel I have nothing to lose except time. I don't have time to wait around, so I just think it's important to take on the toughest challenges. If I fail, then I failed doing the important things, the type of things that, if I succeed, will make great change."

THE BOY WHO BEAT THE BULLET
Aaron Neal

"Stop the car; I've been shot!"

Steve Dance, Young Men president of the Moreland 5th Ward, heard a loud noise and looked in his rearview mirror. Aaron was holding his stomach and writhing in pain. Brother Dance was dubious. He'd spent most of the day with these four rowdy teenage boys. They were returning home after attending the general priesthood meeting in Salt Lake City. The boys were throwing candy at each other and making a mess. Brother Dance was near his wit's end. It was almost eleven at night, and the group was still almost two hours away from home.

Just then fourteen-year-old Aaron screamed, "I'm not kidding." Pleading for someone to believe him, he reached behind his belt and pulled out a piece of shrapnel.

The other boys looked on in terror as Aaron held his stomach and cried, "It hurts so bad!" Brother Dance slammed on the brakes, pulling onto the shoulder of I-15. He quickly jumped out of the van and focused on finding the cause of the damage. As he opened the back door, Brother Dance noted his Coleman cooler was leaking from two holes on opposite sides of the cooler. He also saw the seat covered in foam debris. "I can't believe it," he said. "Someone really did shoot you."

***

October 1, 1988, was a much-anticipated day for Aaron Neal and his teachers quorum. They had planned to spend the day in Salt Lake City and attend the general priesthood meeting that evening.

Steve Dance had volunteered to drive his camper van, hoping the comfortable, pivoting captain seats and other amenities would make the five-hour drive from Blackfoot, Idaho, to Temple Square more enjoyable.

The rowdy young men, dressed in white shirts and ties, had tested Brother Dance's patience. They sat quietly through the meeting, but afterwards, they were eager to shed their ties and burn some of their energy.

They were hungry as well, so they stopped in Bountiful for dinner at Pizza Hut. By nine thirty, they had climbed back in the van and started the long haul home. They were about ten miles from Malad, Idaho, when the boys began throwing candy at one another.

Dirk Martin had thrown a half-eaten Pixie Stix at Aaron. The sugary dust had spilled everywhere—all over Aaron. Not to be outdone, Aaron swiveled his chair around to face the boy, threatening to throw the contents of a *full* Pixie Stix at him. Just as Aaron let it fly, Dirk ducked away, and an unexpected bang rang through the van.

Aaron dropped to the floor, thrashing in pain, but Brother Dance was not convinced. Puzzled, Brother Dance thought he'd blown a tire, but the car was driving normally. Once Aaron produced the copper casing that tipped the slug, it was enough to convince Dance to finally pull over.

Carefully, Brother Dance lifted Aaron's shirt and rolled down the top of his pants to inspect the wound. Just below the belt line was a purple-colored hole about the size of a dime. That brief look at the hole in the young man's stomach sent a shock wave of panic over the driver. He needed to get the boy to a hospital.

Just then the headlights of two oncoming cars approached, slowing to offer assistance. For the first time, Brother Dance noticed his surroundings. Just ahead of where he had pulled off the road, he noticed an idling car. The figures who had begun to walk toward the parked van quickly retreated when the headlights of the other vehicles approached. Brother Dance watched them return to their car, slam the doors, and hit the accelerator. A cloud of dust and gravel was scattered everywhere as they made their getaway. It seemed odd that they had left in such a hurry, but Steve Dance was focused on more pressing matters.

Inside the newly arrived vehicles was Bishop Robert Smith of the Blackfoot 10th Ward, along with others from the ward who had attended the priesthood session. In the second car was the assistant priest quorum advisor and his wife, Carolyn Posegate. Incredibly, she was an emergency room nurse and knew just what to do.

Aaron was growing more and more panicked, fearing that he would die at any moment. Bishop Smith and Brother Dance quickly gave the frightened boy a priesthood blessing. Though the blessing was short, Aaron took comfort in their words: he would stay alive until he could get medical attention.

Amazingly, the wound was not bleeding. They later learned the bullet had punctured the vena cava, a major vein, but for some reason, there was no bleeding. Brother Dance asked Sister Posegate to stay with Aaron while they drove to the hospital. She stayed in the back of the van, pressing her hand onto his wound.

Brother Dance was paralyzed by indecision. Where was the closest hospital? Should he go back to Tremonton? Or was it shorter to go to Pocatello? He headed north for about a mile, then exited the freeway. He drove south toward Tremonton for ten minutes before stopping. Second guessing himself, he decided to head north, back toward Pocatello.

Reaching speeds over ninety miles an hour, the van continued north for another ten minutes. Brother Dance almost lost hope when he saw a sign indicating Pocatello was another fifty miles away. He again pulled off to the side of the road, but this time to bow his head in prayer. "Dear Father in Heaven, please guide me to know where to go."

Pulling back onto the road, he drove north for a few more minutes, finally coming upon the Malad exit. Fortunately, a blue sign directed them toward the nearest hospital. They found the Oneida County Hospital, and Brother Dance ran inside to get help.

After Aaron was loaded onto a stretcher, Sister Posegate finally removed her hand from his stomach, and blood began to gush from the wound. Aaron's clothes were quickly cut off by a nurse while another nurse inserted a large needle to begin a blood transfusion. The doctor almost immediately determined that Aaron would need advanced care in a trauma unit. A medical helicopter was dispatched, and the doctors prepared Aaron to be evacuated to the Bannock Regional Medical Center in Pocatello.

Brother Dance had called Aaron's parents, so when the helicopter arrived in Pocatello, Aaron's father, Gary, was waiting. He watched as Aaron was unloaded and rushed inside. Aaron had already lost over fifty percent of his blood volume and was in extremely critical condition. Although unit after unit of blood was going into his veins, the outlook was grim.

It was one o'clock Sunday morning when Doctor June Hielman rushed into the operating room to scrub-up for surgery. A brief look at the X-rays revealed how badly Aaron had been injured—not only was a major vein damaged but bullet fragments had also damaged his intestines and bowel. The bullet itself was surrounded by a blood clot near his spine, and if left untreated, it could leave Aaron paralyzed. There was much to do and little time before he bled to death.

After three hours of surgery, a nurse emerged from the operating room to explain the unfortunate news. Once the surgeon had opened him up, she had found even more damage than she'd anticipated. The blood clot that formed around the bullet had suddenly burst. They had replaced nearly ten pints of blood and were still unable to stop the bleeding. The nurse didn't believe Aaron would survive.

Dr. Hielman, however, was determined, working on Aaron for another three hours. As soon as she solved one problem, another arose. Discouraged, she set a time limit, committing to continue for just fifteen minutes. If Aaron's condition didn't improve by then, she would stop and pronounce a time of death.

Fifteen minutes passed, then another five minutes. Blood continued oozing from multiple wounds. The assisting surgeon recommended that Dr. Hielman stop, reminding her that she'd done all she could. At this point, even if he did survive, infection would be difficult to overcome. Dr. Heilman looked at the clock on the wall and removed her hands from Aaron's open abdomen.

"I'm going to stop here," she said reluctantly. She was about to pronounce the time of death when Aaron sat up on the operating room table. He looked around at the people in masks and gowns, puzzled. And then, as suddenly as he'd sat up, he lay back down. Dumbfounded, the operating room staff resumed their work. Doctor Heilman looked on with renewed determination.

Another thirty minutes passed, and Dr. Hielman continued her fight to keep Aaron alive. His blood pressure and heart rate fluctuated wildly. His heart rate dropped and didn't bounce back again. Shaking her head in frustration, she again looked at the clock to call time of death.

Just then, she felt a hand on her shoulder, and a man whispered in her ear, "Keep going." When she turned to see who had touched her, no one was near. Despite seeing no evidence of whoever had whispered to her, she continued working.

In eight full hours of surgery, Dr. Heilman had done all she could. Aaron's heart rate and blood pressure had finally stabilized, but his internal organs were being held together by large amounts of surgical silk. Aaron's prognosis was poor. The damage was extensive, and the resultant scar tissue would require additional surgeries, plus months, perhaps an entire year, of hospitalization and rehabilitation.

Amazingly, Aaron's wounds healed quickly. Despite the prediction of a long hospital stay, Aaron was discharged after only fourteen days.

They later learned the cause of the incident: some teens were apprehended for a robbery attempt and admitted their failed plans to rob a van they had shot. Police officials speculated that, had Bishop Smith and Brother and Sister Posegate arrived just thirty seconds later, the van may have already become victims of a robbery, or possibly worse. Surely the timing was quite fortunate, forcing the would-be robbers to abandon their plans. Each faced several criminal charges, and although the gunman was a minor, he was convicted of felonies.

Today, Aaron Neal still suffers from lingering complications related to this incident, but that doesn't stop him from living his life. He is a twenty-year veteran and full-time soldier in the Idaho National Guard. He recently returned from his second tour of duty in Iraq.

Aaron recognizes the unmistakable hand of God in saving his life: "It's pretty amazing that the timing of everything worked out as it did. I'm lucky to be here today."

MYSTERIOUS BLESSINGS
Blake Knight

Every summer, Blake Knight and his wife, Rachelle, hosted her extended family for a reunion at Bear Lake. This beautiful, rustic cabin was bustling with nearly thirty children, teens, and adults.

Wednesday afternoon on July 25, 2012, the kids were lined up behind one another dancing around the sofa. The music blared as they waited for dinner.

Earlier in the day, Blake had asked his brother-in-law to go out on the ATVs with him. Blake had always insisted that everyone ride in pairs. Though his brother-in-law had declined, Blake decided to go anyway. He should have been back by now, and his absence was becoming a concern. By 6 p.m., Rachelle was very worried and suggested someone go look for him. He had been out for several hours. Nobody knew where he was.

***

Enjoying the late summer evening, Blake had ridden for nearly forty-five miles, scouting for the upcoming elk hunt. He was riding at full speed when his ATV inexplicably flipped. Blake was launched headfirst from the vehicle. His head struck the rocky surface, and he bounced several times until he came to a stop. For a moment, Blake was dazed and in pain, then the darkness of unconsciousness enveloped him.

High in the rugged mountains north of Bear Lake, Utah, Blake lay awkwardly next to his ATV. The ring and vibration of his cell phone seemed miles away. Finally, the familiar ringtone startled him from the haze of unconsciousness.

How long have I been out? he thought to himself.

He could hardly see anything with all the caked-on blood covering his eyes and face. His confusion and lack of coordination prevented him from sitting up, but he reached for his phone. As he struggled to focus on the screen, he could see he'd missed five calls from his wife. He looked at the time—6:30. The first call he missed had been nearly twenty minutes earlier. Had he been unconscious that long?

He felt the warmth of his blood dripping down his forehead. He reached clumsily for the back of his head and flinched as his finger slipped deep inside a large gash. Startled, he jerked his hand away. By looking at the pool of blood on the ground, Blake could tell that the amount of blood he'd lost was significant. How he hadn't bled to death was a mystery.

Blake knew he had to get to a doctor, but getting off the mountain seemed almost impossible. He offered a prayer of gratitude that he'd survived and asked for help in getting back to the cabin. As he ended his prayer, he almost immediately regained enough strength to stand. Using the undamaged ATV, he steadied himself, nearly blacking-out again. He held on tight, fighting the dizziness. Within minutes, he could stand on his own.

He started his four-wheeler and looked for an easy path down the hill. Slowly, he inched his way down the steep trail, carefully avoiding the sagebrush and deep ravines. Halfway down the mountain he stopped at a pond to wash the blood from his face before continuing home to the cabin.

After an arduous fifteen-minute ride, he arrived and hastily parked his ATV. Rachelle looked on, eagerly waiting to talk to him. From a distance, she couldn't see the blood that covered his hair and clothing.

"What took you so long?" she asked impatiently. "Why didn't you answer your phone? Is everything okay?"

Blake didn't reply. He unsteadily dismounted the ATV and rushed into the cabin. Bursting through the door, he quickly made his way upstairs to his room, hanging on the railing.

Blake's son, Joston, was in the room. Blake briefly explained what had happened, and Joston helped his dad wash the remaining blood from his face and head. When Rachelle caught up to him, her breath was taken away at the horrific scene.

Blake looked at her calmly. "I've got to go to the hospital, and I don't want anyone to know." He didn't want to make a scene or ruin the reunion for anyone else. He quickly explained what had happened as she hunted for her car keys. After changing his shirt, he was ready to go. He moved quickly but carefully past the other family members and climbed into the passenger's seat, waiting for Rachelle.

As she walked out the door, Rachelle told her sister what had happened and cautioned her to keep it quiet since Blake didn't want anyone to know. The secret was out though, and as soon as the car was gone, the family knelt in prayer, asking a special blessing on Blake.

Bear Lake Community Health Center was only ten minutes away, but the clinic was closed. Fortunately, there was a nurse practitioner inside tending to a patient. Assessing the gash on Blake's head, she told them he would need specialized care. She instructed them to go straight to Logan Regional Hospital to seek proper treatment.

At nine o'clock in the evening, the drive down Logan Canyon would be treacherous. The prospect of facing the steep, winding roads and frequent deer crossings was unsettling. Before they left the clinic, Blake and Rachelle were visited by a few family members, who had gathered to give Blake a priesthood blessing. The blessing offered comfort and reassurance that Blake would be okay. Finally, the couple headed out.

They arrived at the Logan hospital within the hour. He was admitted and hastily escorted to radiology for a CT scan. About an hour after their arrival, Blake and Rachelle listened to the report from the physician.

"The radiologist reviewed your CT scan," the doctor explained, "and we can see no internal or structural damage to your brain due to this accident." Seeing the look of relief the two exchanged, the doctor continued, "However, we did find something unusual that looks like a mass of some sort. It's not related to this accident, but only an MRI can determine what it is." "What do you *think* it is?" Blake queried.

"We don't know. But whatever it is, it's deep into the fourth ventricle. It could be anything from a simple anomaly in the CT scan to a tumor. We're just not sure."

Monday morning, Blake scheduled an MRI. The results were worse than they expected. The MRI showed a tumor the size of a man's pinky finger near Blake's brain stem. He was told that in most cases, tumors in this location were inoperable, but he was referred to the Huntsman Cancer Institute in Salt Lake City, where he met Dr. Randy Jensen.

Dr. Jensen was a neuro-oncologist working as part of the brain tumor research team at the University of Utah and was practicing at the Huntsman facility. Blake was scheduled for surgery the following week.

A flood of prayers were offered on Blake's behalf. Blake's ward as well as his family and friends held a special fast. The outpouring of love was almost tangible, and it helped sustain Blake and his family during this trying time.

The surgery was grueling. The team worked for over eight hours just to expose the brain stem. One mistake could have paralyzed or killed the patient. Working agonizingly slowly, the doctors finally uncovered the large, white tumor. They carefully peeled away the surrounding tissue and latched on to the tumor. Most of it slipped out without much effort, and only a few remnants had to be manually extricated.

The surgery was successful, and though the tumor turned out to be benign, Dr. Jensen reported that it still could have killed Blake. In fact, had they not found the tumor when they did, within a matter of days or maybe weeks, Blake would have experienced what Dr. Jensen called "a catastrophic event."

His life had been spared, but the recovery was not easy. He experienced debilitating double vision and vertigo, making it impossible for him to work. The financial and emotional tolls were significant. A full seven months after the initial surgery, doctors recommended another surgery to relieve the symptoms.

During this procedure, surgeons discovered another unrelated issue that could only have been discovered and treated by surgery. The retina in Blake's right eye was nearly detached, and if not immediately repaired, it would have caused blindness. His symptoms quickly became manageable, and shortly after this second surgery, Blake was able to drive and resume most of his day-to-day activities.

Looking back, the hand of the Lord was unmistakable during this entire ordeal. First, Blake had survived the gash to his head and bleeding profusely for nearly twenty minutes. But were it not for the accident, he would likely have died from the results of a tumor in the far reaches of his brain. Had that not resulted in double vision and required surgery, he most likely would have gone blind in one eye. Blake's incident turned out to be an incredible blessing.

A MOTHER'S LOVE

Kitty de Ruyter-Bons

I was born in Semarang, on the island of Java, in the Dutch East Indies, now known as Indonesia. The Indonesian islands curl along the Equator like a string of pearls—south of the Philippines, north of Australia, and east and west of Singapore.

Like Nephi of old, I too came from goodly parents. In my youth, I was taught to love God and have faith in him, and I saw how the scriptures came to life because of examples of righteous living.

My mother, Anna Johannes van Burg, did not have an easy life. Her father, Johannes van Burg, was Dutch; her mother, Karsih, was a native Javanese. In those days, in the Dutch East Indies where they lived, the government would not recognize marriage between a Dutch citizen and a native woman of the colonies. Her father traveled extensively, and she could not live with her mother, as it was unthinkable for a Euro-Asian child to live with her mother in a native village. So Anna was boarded out with a good Christian Indo family by the name of Worthington so that she could be raised as a European child.

My mother was soft-spoken and always hummed a song or hymn as she worked. I never heard her utter a profane word of any kind. She had fair skin inherited from her Dutch father and soft, fawn-like brown eyes. She preferred to wear her naturally wavy, dark brown hair cut short and parted in the middle.

Mams loved beauty and surrounded us with it. We began each day in beauty, gathering in our dining room for prayers and breakfast. My mother loved plants and flowers, so the dining room held palms, ming trees, and other ornamental plants. An abundance of flowers decorated the sideboard and each of the round tables in the sitting area in front of the bay windows. The china always glistened, the crystal sparkled, and the silverware shone. The napkins were artfully folded like fans on the plates.

Since my mother had earned her pharmacist's certificate as a young woman, the people in the village lovingly called her Bonda Bomo or Ibu Doktor, meaning "mother the doctor." Mams healed a village baby from malaria when the holy man from the village had given up. Another time, a tree fell on Si Sudarman, our gardener, during a severe thunderstorm, and his legs were crushed. My mother was summoned to the village, where she set his legs as best she could. My mother nursed him back to health and taught his mother to massage his legs so that he could walk again using crutches.

There were many of these stories, and the people truly believed that my mother had healing hands.

Each of the children had a private baboe, or nanny. My nanny was Baboe Kit. Baboe Kit was not young. I often tried to picture her without the wrinkles around her eyes and mouth, and saw that she must have been a beautiful woman in her younger days. Her long hair was neatly knotted at the back of her head, with a big pin made of teakwood keeping it in place.

Baboe Kit was a very wise woman, and in my eyes she could do no wrong. She was a Muslim by faith, as are most of the island inhabitants. My family was Christian, so my mother counseled me to think of my Heavenly Father when my nanny would speak of Allah, and to think of the Lord Jesus Christ when she spoke of the prophet Mohammed. Both my mother and my nanny taught me to love God and to obey Him.

It was the custom in our home to start the day with a prayer, a scripture reading, a song, and a thought before breakfast was served. Everyone was expected to attend and be on time. Each morning my father read to us from the Bible to teach us a concept or quality to emulate. His favorite book was John, perhaps because he had been named after this disciple.

After breakfast, all the children attended school. We lived near our coffee plantation on the mountain, so there were no public schools nearby. My parents hired tutors to teach the smaller children at home, but the older ones had to travel forty-five miles to the city to attend middle and high schools.

***

When Japan attacked Pearl Harbor on December 7, 1941, my idyllic life on the island changed dramatically. The Japanese needed oil and had already defeated the Americans in the Philippines, so we fully expected a Japanese invasion. The government of the Dutch East Indies declared a state of emergency.

We were no match for the Japanese troops, who quickly overcame our military forces and placed all military personnel behind barbed wire and all Europeans in concentration camps to prevent any acts of sabotage. My father was able to elude the Japanese for a long time. The Japanese decided to use his family to persuade him to give himself up, and we were put under house arrest.

It was during this time that my mother gave birth to my youngest brother. She prepared herself well for this event, even boiling the water beforehand. My sister Annalise had assisted my mother and was proudly beaming from ear to ear. My new little brother was given the name Dieudonne William (which means "given by God"). We called him Wim.

Mams suspected that we would be sent to a prison camp, and she prepared us for this eventuality. Using pillow cases, she sewed packs for each of us children and herself. The packs even had handles so we could carry them on our backs. She packed them with dried fruit, dried meat similar to jerky, a hand towel, a toothbrush, a comb, and soap, as well as a set of clean underwear and outer clothing made out of the sturdiest material she could find. Mams also kept her black pharmacist's bag well stocked with medicines, bandages, razor blades, medical instruments, scissors, and a sewing kit, as well as two hair clippers, which she used to give haircuts to the village children.

It was on a rainy day, when the water seemed to pour out of the heavens in buckets, that we received the news that my father had been captured. A Japanese officer came into our quarters, and Mother was taken to Semarang, the capital of mid-Java, where the bank had been converted into military headquarters. She was interrogated before being allowed to spend a few minutes with my father, who had also been interrogated and still showed signs of having been beaten. They had only a few tender moments before she was led away.

Only a few days later, the Japanese came to take all of us to concentration camps. My mother had replenished our backpacks with dried food and packed two large suitcases with our clothes and other belongings.

The soldiers came very early in the morning, and I was too sleepy to think clearly; consequently, I left my favorite toy—Pop Mientje, my rag doll—behind. My mother had given me instructions to be in charge of her black medical bag, and in my haste I had grabbed my backpack and the black bag, but left my rag doll behind.

Mams approached the sentry in charge and said, "We have not yet had the chance to say our morning prayers. It would be most beneficial to the boys to receive a blessing from God." They gave their permission, and we were allowed to have this last family prayer, in which my mother invoked the Lord's choicest blessings to be with her boys and to protect them.

"Bless our captors, dear Lord, and soften their hearts so they will use mercy and kindness as they deal with our family," she continued. And then she asked an individual blessing on each of her sons.

She reminded the boys to remember her teachings for survival and to guard the articles in their backpacks. Later, Mams told us that she had put one bag of salt and one bag of money in each of the boys' backpacks. People in camps would sell their food, and the native Indonesians would provide food for money or would barter for salt.

Saying good-bye was difficult because we realized that we might never see each other again. It was especially heartbreaking for Mams. She knew their chances of survival. Bravely, she embraced and kissed her sons, whispering softly special words to each. Konrad and Daniel were put in a small truck together. Herbie was placed in a second vehicle.

My mother, the baby, and we girls were led to a third truck. As we rode slowly through the village, many of our neighbors and friends saw us and waved. We saw Baboe Kit and our faithful houseboy, Resoh, at a distance. They courteously bowed their heads and waved. Observing all the people of the village who had gathered to pay homage to her, my mother looked about her, as if taking a photograph of this scene.

We were taken to a concentration camp, where we encountered friends we didn't recognize because of the changes that had come over them through hunger and disease. It was hot and humid, and the stench was horrible. Our barracks were infested with flies, lice, roaches, rats, and mosquitoes.

We were each allowed one and a half meters of space on the dirt floor. Because we had brought blankets, we didn't have to sleep on the dirty mats that were provided for us. Mams was even able to fashion our mosquito nets over our sleeping area with poles driven into the ground to protect us from the ever-troublesome mosquitoes. After we had been assigned our spot, Mams saw an older woman lying asleep in a corner on the damp dirt floor. She had nothing to lie on.

"Ellen, Kitty," Mams turned to us, "would you share a blanket, so this woman need not lie in the dirt?" She walked over to the old woman and offered her our blanket. The woman was too ill or too weak to respond, so Mams picked her up and gently arranged the blanket beneath her.

While in this camp, we continued to have prayer each morning to thank Heavenly Father for food and water and for our lives. Since it was forbidden to display any form of religion, we had to get up very early in order to be able to kneel and say our prayers. Always we asked the Lord to watch over the boys and my father and to sustain them in their hour of need.

"Why are you so foolish to risk your lives to pray to a God who does not seem to hear us or care about us?" our prisonmates asked. "If He cared, would we be in this terrible place?"

Mother calmly ignored the disparaging remarks of others and continued to teach us of peaceable things. She had no Bible, but her memory of its teachings was phenomenal. Each morning after prayers, Mams reminded us that we were to "love your enemies, bless them that curse you, do good to them that hate you, and pray for them that despitefully use you and persecute you" (Matthew 5:44–45).

She taught us that because we had little food and water, our energy level would be very low. If we were to use this little energy that we had to hate our enemies, to hate our environment, and to hate the people around us, that hate would consume this little energy and get us nowhere. But if we were to use this energy to love our God first and to love those around us, or at least to see the good in them, love would enhance our character.

Our mother would draw the camp children around her for Bible storytelling, especially when we were forced to watch the Japanese abuse the prisoners. To shield us from the atrocities, she would place herself in front of us and say, "I think that you children would prefer to hear a story about Jesus rather than watching these awful things." Then she would sit down on the ground and begin to tell the stories. Many other children would sit down with us and listen, fascinated.

My mother had been appointed our barracks spokesperson, and one day it fell upon her to provide twenty-eight young women between the ages of fourteen and twenty-two to be used as prostitutes for the Japanese, who were celebrating a holiday. She took the problem to the Lord.

She fasted and prayed, and was finally inspired to shave all the hair of some sixty young women with the scissors, razor blades, sharp medical instruments, and hair clippers from her medical bag, which was never taken away from her.

To prevent the guards from discovering her plan, she had to wait until after work detail. This meant that she had exactly three and a half minutes to do all of this. Although Mams asked for volunteers to help, only six others dared to come forward to help save the girls.

Mams also passed the girls pieces of a plant she had found growing near the barbed wire fence. Because of her knowledge of herbs and plants, she knew that the sap would give off a noxious odor when it touched human skin, so she encouraged the girls to smear the sap all over their bodies. This would make them doubly unappealing to the Japanese officers.

At the appointed time, there stood some sixty foul-smelling girls with shaven heads waiting for the Japanese who had come to claim their prize. Punishment for the guilty was inevitable, as this was an open revolt.

The Japanese took turns screaming insults at us and slapping the women. At last, they took my mother and the others who had helped her and stood them before the crowd. Then they ripped the women's clothing off, ridiculing and shaming them. It was a horrible scene.

One officer pointed to my mother. "Why have you done this wrong against the officers of the Japanese Imperial Forces?" he demanded. "You have been appointed to be a barracks unit leader. You must set an example of obedience." He made the mistake of placing a bullhorn to her mouth for her response, and she took the opportunity to testify how she had found the courage for what she had done.

"My God has sanctified some things in our lives," she said. "Virtue is one of these. As a Christian people, we have been commanded to live virtuous lives. We will protect this virtue at all costs, even unto death. I will take responsibility for the action that I have taken."

This reply infuriated the Japanese, who slapped my mother about the face until blood flowed from her nose and mouth. Then they bound her against a pole with her hands over her head. "So you are a Christian?" they asked her. "Are you willing to die for this cause?"

"I am," she answered. Again they slapped her as they continued to ask questions. Soon a samurai sword was drawn, and as we had witnessed beheadings before, we thought she would surely be beheaded. Instead, the man used his sword to cut a cross on her bare back. A samurai sword is razor-sharp, its cuts deep and painful.

The officer nicked my mother a few times on her arms. The beatings began again, this time with belts. The buckle of one belt became stuck where the two cuts of the cross met, ripping a piece of flesh from my mother's back. My sweet mother remained silent; she seemed to have full control over her body.

When at last the officers cut her loose, she lost her balance and fell. As she slowly got to her knees, one officer kicked her, and she fell backward. Again she got to her knees then to her feet, where she stood erect, her head high. The officers dismissed the other women and proclaimed a punishment for the ringleader. Mother was sentenced to two weeks in the pit.

The pits were nine- to ten-foot-deep holes in the ground where one could stand or squat but never lie down because the pits were not wide enough. The tops were covered with chicken wire and fastened on all sides. Food and water were thrown into the pit. One had to stand in one's own filth. Usually those sentenced to the pit did not survive.

The sentence was pronounced, and my mother's eyes sought her children in the multitude as she beckoned us to come to her. Mams bent down to our level and looked each of us in the eyes. Her eyes were tearless as she asked us to remain faithful and to sustain her with our prayers. "Now I need you children to be brave and to continue to get up early in the morning to pray to our Heavenly Father," she said. "Thank Him for the blessings of life. Ask Him to continue to bless you, to watch over you, and to keep you safe. Then ask Him to have mercy on me and to bless me with inner strength so that I may survive this ordeal and come back to you."

Before we could kiss her or say good-bye, she was led away.

The first night alone in the camp without our mother was a frightening experience. We rearranged ourselves in our sleeping area; Annalise took my mother's place, with the baby and Ellen on each side of her.

Without our mother to care for us, obtaining food was a problem. Annalise fiercely defended our position when standing in line to receive our food, determined to take care of us all by herself. There was no peace in our hearts, just fear and anxiety.

Through the grace of the Lord, my mother survived her ordeal. It was a tremendously happy moment when we heard the shouting that my mother had been released and saw her walk slowly towards us, her arms open, inviting us to come to her.

Mams took the time to greet the many women who came forward to welcome her, yet I knew that she must have been in great pain. Her legs and feet were swollen to at least three times their normal size, and she looked utterly exhausted. Her lips were blistered and her eyes swollen from being exposed to the elements for such a long period of time.

Mams was led towards our barracks and into the washing area, where it was discovered that her body had already begun to rot. We took live maggots from her back and lovingly washed her with water contributed by the women in the barracks, who had sacrificed their washing water for her.

Water was a very precious commodity, and we were allowed only one basin of washing water each week. Many of the women suffered from diseases and needed the water to quench their thirst or to keep their fever down, yet they sacrificed their water to bathe my mother.

After Mams was washed and dressed in clean clothes, her first act was to go on her knees in the open for everyone to see, defying the prohibition of any expression of religion. She was especially thankful to Heavenly Father for preserving her life by sending rain. It had rained three times during this usually dry season, and she was able to collect clean water by scraping dirt down from the wall of her pit to create a shelf for her drinking cup to stand on. In this manner she could catch this rainwater so that it would not mingle with the filth in the bottom of the pit. At midday, a breeze would come, moving branches from a nearby tree to shade her, giving her some relief from the hot tropical sun. To us this was a manifestation that there was indeed a Heavenly Father who was mindful of our plight, who had heard our petitions and had answered our prayers and sent our mother back to us.

We had been in the camp about three months when I had my ninth birthday and received an unexpected visitor. I had wandered away from the barracks in search of fresh air and was just standing at the outskirts of the compound when I heard my name called. I knew immediately that it was my nanny. Looking around anxiously, I finally saw her, sitting in the underbrush and smiling at me.

"Oh, Baboe Kit, have you come to take me away from this awful place?" I asked.

"No, my child," came the familiar voice. "I have come to give you something because today is your birthday!"

Pretending to play with my stick in case any Japanese soldiers should see me, I edged closer to her. "Baboe Kit," I pleaded, "please, take me with you. I hate it here."

"Shh . . . ," she admonished me sternly. "You must keep your voice down. Now listen. I have walked a great distance and waited here at the gate for many days to see you. I have your doll. You left her behind when you were taken, and she wants to be here with you. Remember to say your prayers," she continued. "Ask for strength and endurance, and be obedient, and Allah's spirit will be with you and protect you. This too shall pass. Perhaps there is a purpose for which you need to go through these bad times. Remember, there is to be opposition in all things, to have to taste of the bitter to savor the sweet things in life, to be hungry to appreciate an abundance of food, to be held captive to cherish and protect freedom.

"I know it is not your destiny to die in this camp. Take this doll, protect her, and she will bring you comfort." She told me to turn toward the holy city of Mecca and swear that I would take care of the doll.

I shifted my position then crawled closer to the barbed wire. I had learned to be obedient, but this time the need for her touch was too great. When she handed me the doll, our hands touched, and she stroked my hand. Again, I pleaded, "Oh please, Nanny, take me with you!" I threw the doll aside, reaching out for her with both hands and cutting my face on the barbed wire as I attempted to press my body closer. I closed my eyes, savoring the feeling of her arms around me and her soft hands wiping away my tears.

She whispered a few words then suddenly and urgently said, "I must go now. Go quickly and take your doll!" She pulled back, but I could not let her go. I could not see, as she did, the sentry who was coming toward us. As I held onto my nanny for one last second, the sentry saw us. Thinking that she was escaping from the camp, he took aim and fired.

A gaping, bloody wound appeared in my nanny's back. She turned to face me and smiled as if to tell me that it was all right. Then she fell to the ground. I stood in shock, watching my nanny die, hearing her cry.

It was of course my mother who found me, clutching my doll against me. Instantly, she knew that I had seen my nanny, and she folded me into her arms as she gently led me away. "Nanny must have known she would be risking her life to come here, but she came because she loved you. She knew that you missed your rag doll and wanted to bring her to you."

Then I understood the true meaning of the Bible scripture that said, "Greater love hath no man than this, that a man lay down his life for his friends" (John 15:13).

***

In time, the war ended, but the Indonesian government had confiscated all of our property. We moved to Holland, where my father died from complications of his injuries. To my mother fell the task of raising our family alone.

Because of the prejudice against the Indos, Mother's pharmacist certificate from the Dutch East Indies was not valid. She was forced to look for other avenues of employment and eventually found work in a small factory. After work, she hooked huge Smyrna carpets on consignment for the owner of the factory or its wealthy clients.

We had been living in Holland for about a year and a half when Mams asked me to stay home from school one day. I was surprised by the request, knowing how Mams felt about us attending school.

Mams paced back and forth in the little living room, then she started to cry. I had never seen my mother cry—not when she was tortured, not when she heard the news about the death of her son, not even when her husband died. I knew that something was wrong.

"Oh, my God, where are you?" Mams whimpered. "Have you forsaken us?" She showed me a letter from the landlord, who had raised the rent again with a warning that if she did not come up with the new rent, we would be evicted. Mams had no idea where this extra money was to come from. She was on the brink of despair.

I asked if we could have a prayer together, so we knelt down. I do not remember what I voiced to our Heavenly Father, but we both felt calmed. Needing comfort, I reached for Pop Mientje, my rag doll. To my horror, I suddenly realized how dirty my doll was; after all, she had been through a lot with me.

I decided to clean her, but as I scrubbed her face, the material disintegrated. I reached into the stuffing of the doll to arrange it properly but found far more than the soft cotton the doll was made of. To my amazement, she spilled forth a treasure she had carried all these years—sapphires, diamonds, rubies, pearls, jade, and gold rings!

These were some of the jewels my mother had entrusted to my nanny, Baboe Kit, and the other servants before we were put under house arrest. Our servants were to use the jewels as they saw fit, perhaps even to save their own families from hunger.

After the Japanese had taken us away, Baboe Kit must have gone back to our house. There she discovered my rag doll. Knowing how important it was to me, she must have devised the plan to take the larger and more valuable stones and carefully sew them into my rag doll. The doll she would then bring to me—an act that had cost her her life.

When I showed my mother the jewelry, she immediately fell to the floor and knelt in prayer, asking Heavenly Father to forgive her for her lack of faith. She should have known that He would never forsake her. Her prayer of thanksgiving lasted a long time.

SNOWBOUND

Josh Holdaway

WHILE JOSH HOLDAWAY STRUGGLED TO free his snowmobile in Utah's backcountry, he thought back on the events that had led him to this moment. Today, December 31, was the final day of Josh's snowmobiling trip. The four-day trip had been a Christmas present from his parents. His father had arranged to use a neighbor's cabin in the Uinta Mountains.

The conditions were perfect for the much-anticipated winter adventure, not that Josh knew much about that. The eighteen-year-old was relatively new to the powerful snowmobiles, and his six-foot-three frame, which had helped him earn a spot on the Bingham High School basketball team, prevented him from growing too comfortable on the machine. He could barely manage to fold himself into the seat and still towered over the windshield. As he rode, the frigid wind bit at his head and shoulders.

Josh and his father were accompanied by four other neighbors and friends who each had years of experience with snowmobiling. Josh was amazed at how some of them could push their machines to the limit—speeding through potentially dangerous areas. Due in part to his greenness, Josh was hesitant to take big risks, and he was inevitably left behind until someone backtracked to find him.

Over the last three days, Josh had become more familiar with the snowmobiles. He had grown to enjoy the outings in the crisp mountain air, so on this last day, the group had ventured far beyond the familiar surroundings to a remote area. Exploring virgin powder on the open hillsides was a dream for the skilled men, but Josh was happy to follow in their tracks. Doing so helped him keep up with his group, especially through the thick, wooded areas.

It had been a good day, but by three o'clock, the men began to make their way back to the cabin. They seemed in a bit of a hurry to return to the cabin and pack up. Josh was proud that, finally, he was not the last man in the group. But the snow and cold were unrelenting, and the growing numbness in his fingers and toes told him he needed to readjust his helmet and snowsuit.

Just as he stopped his snowmobile, Josh watched the last man in their party roar by. The man smiled and waved at Josh, clearly enjoying the last moments of their vacation. Josh felt a wave of urgency to continue, not wanting to lose sight of his friends. After quickly checking his snow gear, he pressed the accelerator. Josh pushed the machine faster than he normally would have dared, hot in pursuit. After several anxious moments, Josh knew it was in vain. He simply couldn't keep up; he had lost sight of the group.

Frustrated, he continued to follow the tracks, weaving through a maze of winding trails through the forest of snow-covered trees. It wasn't until he reached a clearing where the trail branched off in several directions that Josh decided he would have to wait. He wasn't sure which trail would lead him back to the cabin and figured that someone would come back to find him, as they had on the previous days. The minutes dragged on. Josh looked at the sky through the trees; the sunlight was fading fast, and there couldn't even be an hour of daylight left. Soon the sun, and what warmth it provided, would be completely hidden.

Fighting the rising panic, Josh tried to think. Hoping to hear the others' engines, he turned his machine off. Ten, twenty, thirty minutes passed, and still, he heard nothing. After forty-five minutes, it was clear that he could wait no longer. No one was coming back for him. Alarmed, he glanced at the numerous trails in front of him. Which should he pick? He had to decide, had to take a chance. Choosing a trail he thought looked vaguely familiar, he started his snowmobile and rode for several minutes. Suddenly, he felt a surge of hope—a trail he recognized.

He aimed his machine up the hill, but after a steep climb, the promising trail came to an abrupt dead end. Trying to back track, Josh made a horrific discovery—his snowmobile wouldn't budge. The snowmobile sputtered, and Josh stood to get off the machine. Stepping into the snow, he sunk until he was almost completely submerged. He clung desperately to the seat handle to keep himself from sinking farther into the fresh powder. He stepped repeatedly, trying to compact the snow beneath him in order to get some leverage to climb back onto the snowmobile.

"I have to get this thing turned around," he kept saying to himself. Every effort to do so, however, met with failure. He tried to lift the front of the sled. He tried prying it out with a stick. A search of the machine's compartments turned up only a useless piece of twine. The impossibility of the situation weighed on him, and he took off his helmet and threw it at the unyielding snowmobile.

A cry of part frustration, part fear escaped into the ever-increasing darkness. The prospect of being stranded overnight loomed. Fighting his feelings of dread, he sunk to his knees in the wet snow and prayed. It was his final hope, his only option. He was stuck without shelter or provisions in sub-zero weather. Without God's help, Josh knew he would not survive the night.

***

Little did Josh know, that at that moment his father was also praying. When it was obvious Josh was lost, a sense of urgency and fear set in. Josh's mother and siblings traveled to the cabin to help with the search effort. Both parents had a constant plea in their hearts for their son's safety. Their despair almost overwhelmed them.

They had called emergency services, and a virtual army of volunteers sprang into action. Men and women abandoned their warm houses in search of a boy lost in the bitter winter night. They searched diligently, but most had to push aside fears that a teenager could survive a night like this. A man's body had been found a few weeks earlier—he had died in the same mountains, in temperatures just barely below zero, after only eight hours. Even an experienced outdoorsman couldn't endure the current temperature, nearly forty degrees below zero. Josh's chances did not look good.

***

A feeling of peace enveloped Josh as he stood from his prayer. With renewed determination, he summoned the energy to walk. He was headed for the trees, the only shelter he knew. With each step, the snow grew deeper. With each step, Josh sunk deeper, and his new-found determination waned. At one point, he became completely submerged. With a great effort that sapped the last of his energy, Josh was able to pull himself out of the hole, only to collapse in a heap of fatigue. Breathing heavily, he looked helplessly toward heaven and sobbed uncontrollably. "I don't want to die. I don't want to die." His plea unheard by human ears.

Gathering himself together, Josh realized he had no time to waste—he had to find shelter. He looked at a clump of trees where the snow was not so deep, but there was nothing to use for shelter. The pain in his hands and feet was getting worse. Though he wore insulated mittens and socks, his hands grew numb in the sub-zero temperature. He wiggled his fingers and toes, trying to retain what little feeling he still had. He was losing control of his muscles. He shivered with such intensity that it was hard to breathe.

He stumbled into a clearing, looking for a comfortable place to sleep. He noticed a fallen tree and hoped he could rest there, but unable to walk another step, he fell to the ground in a daze. Time slowed to a crawl.

He had lost all hope of surviving the night. He was prepared to die, to end the pain. He thought of his parents. Would they feel guilty for having given him this trip as a gift? He hoped not. He didn't want to hurt his parents. What would happen to them? With no one else to turn to, he prayed aloud.

"Dear Heavenly Father, if I die tonight, please watch over my family. Let them know I love them and tell them not to worry about me."

The familiar peace washed over him. Suddenly, though, it was more than that—he felt a distinct presence. It was Grandfather Hunter. He had come to be with Josh in this time of extreme need. Josh had no doubt that it was his grandpa. The presence was palpable and unmistakable. Josh felt a wave of warmth come over him, and he was embraced by an intense feeling of love.

Is this what dying felt like? Is this what it's like to be in the presence of angels? He was comforted knowing he wasn't alone. While his grandfather was alive, Josh had developed a special bond with him. As the oldest grandchild, Josh had made many special memories with his grandfather. It had been a shock when, only a few months earlier, Grandpa had passed away. He had only been sixty-three and was looking forward to a long retirement to spend time with his family. It had been on Josh's birthday, and it had broken his heart to have to say good-bye to his beloved grandfather.

At the time, he hadn't understood why God had taken his grandfather, but now it all made perfect sense. He could put all the pieces together. He realized the wisdom of God's plan. Having Grandpa with him at this critical moment meant Josh didn't feel cheated at all. What a great blessing it turned out to be. Had his grandfather still been alive, he wouldn't have been there when Josh needed him most. Through his death, he was able to bless Josh at this critical time. It reminded Josh that his Heavenly Father was aware of his dire situation and had known precisely how to lend His comfort and love. Josh thought to himself that it was okay to die. All he wanted was to stop shaking.

In his confused and frightened state, Josh had left his helmet where it had fallen by the snowmobile. This meant he had no protection for his ears, nose, and face. Josh did his best to burrow under a snow-covered log. His only hope was to die quickly. The unmistakable presence of heavenly beings put him completely at ease. He was ready. He could no longer fight the urge to sleep. He closed his eyes and all sense of time seemed to drift away.

The first morning of the new year dawned cold but clear in the Uinta Mountains. Josh had been lost for nearly eighteen hours when he was startled awake by the heat of the sun on his face. Disoriented, he remembered hearing noises during the night. He thought he may have also seen flashes from headlights of snowmobiles. After a moment, Josh came fully to his senses. He was alive. He tried to shake the last of the confusion from his mind. His body was completely numb. He knew he needed to get help. After several failed and painful attempts, Josh was finally able to stand, and he began to make his way through the snow.

It wasn't long before he heard a helicopter. The sound seemed to be coming closer. Josh stopped to listen closer. When he saw the helicopter's rotors, he turned toward it and fumbled closer. This was his chance. He had to make them see him, but his weakened legs could not carry him far before he needed to stop and rest. He exerted all his energy to yell as loud as he could. Finally, the distinctive red and white helicopter hovered directly in front of him.

As soon as Josh knew the helicopter crew had seen him, the last of his reserves gave out. He collapsed to the snow and sobbed. His body was so numb that he barely noticed the blizzard of snow created by the aircraft. He didn't feel the sting of the icy crystals as the helicopter landed. He couldn't feel anything.

Josh was relieved to see a paramedic climb from the helicopter and rush to his aid. He helped Josh into the aircraft, and as soon as the sliding door had closed, the chopper rose above the snow-covered trees.

Josh watched out the window as they passed above the grove where he had lived out that terrifying ordeal. However, what he felt was not terror but reverence for his own sacred grove. It was holy because Grandpa Hunter and a cadre of angels had protected him throughout the night.

He felt a surge of gratitude for the love he had felt and for the better understanding he had gained. He knew that he was only alive because of the divine intervention of a loving Heavenly Father.

He then spotted his abandoned snowmobile. It was only a few hundred feet from where he had spent the night. Had he really only walked that far? It had felt so much farther. The thought brought another wave of gratitude.

While he watched out the window, the paramedics assessed him for injuries. There were no broken bones or cuts, but they knew the consequences of the cold would be serious. Josh turned away from the window to watch as they carefully peeled the frozen mittens from his hands. It was frightening that he couldn't even feel their hands on his own. His dream of playing college basketball could be in jeopardy.

The paramedic recognized the signs of frostbite. Josh's skin was grayish-yellow. His fingers were frozen solid and couldn't be manipulated. The skin looked like it was made of translucent wax. He could sense Josh's fear and tried to avoid answering the boy's question, "Are my hands going to be okay?"

After a short but bumpy ride, the rescue chopper landed at LDS Hospital in Salt Lake City, where Josh was immediately rushed to the trauma unit. Nurses and aides helped Josh out of his wet clothing and wrapped him in blankets. They were careful not to warm him too quickly either.

As his body began to thaw, Josh noticed doctors standing near, whispering to one another. They were dumbfounded at seeing no frostbite on Josh's head. It was completely inexplicable. He had spent the night with no shelter and no covering for his head. With the windchill, the temperature had been recorded at thirty-eight below zero. Surely such extreme conditions should have caused severe frostbite. Josh had somehow escaped any disfiguring damage to his face.

It took Josh's father and brother nearly two hours to get to the hospital to see Josh. Besides the company they offered, they had brought consecrated oil and gave Josh the first of many priesthood blessings. Their words comforted Josh and reaffirmed their love. They specifically told him he would not lose the use of his hands.

A few hours later, the attention turned from Josh's hands to his feet. Josh screamed in sheer agony as his tender feet were placed in tubs of lukewarm water. The stabbing pain was like being poked by millions of needles. Soon his feet began to swell and weep a clear fluid. The constant pain prevented Josh from putting any weight on his feet. Each time he tried to stand, an unbearable shock wave of pain swept through his body.

After a few days, the toes on both of his feet had turned black. His left foot was farther blackened with dead tissue, past the arch on his foot. It was clear that his toes, as well as part of his foot, would have to be amputated. Josh was heartbroken as he pondered the effect that would have on his future. While he knew that his toes could not be saved, he held onto the promise that his hands would be spared.

But after several weeks, it looked like that was a vain hope. Several doctors recommended that Josh's hands be amputated. Josh and his family clung to the hope that had come from that first priesthood blessing. They requested doctor after doctor to assess Josh's frostbitten hands. They wanted to hear about options for surgery or rehabilitation, and they were disappointed to hear each doctor recommend that his hands should be amputated at the wrist.

The news was devastating, but Josh and his family stood firm. They continued to search for an answer to their prayers, for a way the blessing could be fulfilled. Finally, their diligence and faith triumphed when Dr. Laird Swensen, an orthopedic surgeon, was called to consult. Dr. Swensen had learned of a new technique developed in China. It was considered an experimental procedure. No US doctors had successfully attempted the technique, but Josh was adamant. He had nothing to lose.

The day before the surgery was scheduled, Josh had a feeling that he was going to be visited by Thomas S. Monson, then the second counselor in the First Presidency of The Church of Jesus Christ of Latter-day Saints. No one had called to schedule the visit, but Josh told his family of his inspiration. He was so confident that he even joked to his parents that he had better wash his hair to be ready to greet President Monson.

**

President Monson called the pharmacy at LDS Hospital and confirmed that the items he needed were in stock. Typically, he had an assistant take care of these matters, but for some reason he decided to handle it himself that day. The woman at the pharmacy (who actually happened to be Josh's cousin) offered to have the items delivered. He thanked her but said he was going to be in the area and would just come pick them up.

A short time later, he arrived in the pharmacy, and a conversation ensued. The discussion ended when she mentioned that her cousin Josh was upstairs. President Monson recalled hearing about Josh on the news and offered to go visit him.

***

As Josh was returning to his room after a treatment in the hyperbaric chamber, he noticed a commotion near his room. When Josh was wheeled inside, President Monson exclaimed, "I'm glad you're here!" They chatted briefly, then President Monson offered to give Josh a priesthood blessing in anticipation of the upcoming surgery. Josh was thrilled and eagerly accepted the offer.

The room grew quiet and somber as President Monson laid his hands on Josh's head and pronounced the blessing. He stated emphatically, "The Lord has held you in the palm of His hands. You are alive for a reason, and He will bless you to get through this."

After the visit, Josh's attitude changed dramatically. He had been terribly discouraged, but now he no longer felt sorry for himself. Now he knew that he had an important mission yet to accomplish.

The surgery lasted an incredible twelve hours, and it was only the first of more than twenty surgeries Josh would undergo to regain the use of his hands. Eventually, he regained nearly all the function he had prior to the incident.

Today, Josh is a licensed clinical social worker for Valley Mental Health in Salt Lake City. He is a specialized case worker who helps homeless clients obtain shelter and the mental health services they need. During the winter, he can often be found walking the frosty streets of the city looking for people to rescue from the cold. He is grateful to be uniquely qualified for his chosen career, but above all, he is grateful to have been allowed to experience a brief glimpse of heaven. It has given him an eternal perspective.

THE BULLET AND THE BOOK OF MORMON

DARWIN SMITH

THE DRONE OF ANIMALS AND insects native to this tropical rainforest was an annoyance. It interfered with Darwin's highly attuned senses. Darwin Smith, 18, of Ashton, Idaho, was leading his unit on a search and clear mission trying to rid the area of enemy fighters.

This was what he had trained for, but with each step, the eerie feeling of déjà vu grew stronger. His heart pounded loudly in his chest. He continued on, gripping his rifle tightly while cautiously scanning the trees for any signs of danger.

Suddenly, it dawned on him—he knew why this place was so familiar. He had seen it in a dream or, to be precise, many dreams. It was the place from the terrifying nightmares he'd endured for an entire week during his special forces training. It all seemed so surreal. He had been warned about this moment. And now he was overwhelmed by a feeling of impending doom. Trying to shake the oppressive sensation he thought, *This is nuts. I've never been here before. This is all just in my head.*

The fog of his dream-like memory was lifted, and he began to panic.

"Get out of here," he whispered to himself—but it was too late. Just like in his dream, when he rounded the corner, his chest was engulfed in a stinging pain, and a loud BOOM disturbed the jungle. His chest felt as though it would explode, and he was dazed by the intensity of the pain. Lying on his back, he watched the canopy of trees fade into darkness and listened to the burst of gunfire his unit directed at the source of the shot.

With a thud, the enemy sniper fell head-first from the tree not fifty yards from where Darwin had stood. The men in the platoon broke off in all directions to search for other threats, but after a few tense minutes, the all-clear sounded.

***

Darwin Smith had just finished nearly ten months of arduous military training and was looking forward to returning home on a long awaited furlough. He arrived at his home in Idaho the week of Thanksgiving 1967. He and his unit were scheduled to arrive in Vietnam just after the first of the new year. After boot camp, Darwin had been selected to receive Special Forces training with the Green Berets, the Army's elite group of highly skilled soldiers. During that training, he had also been privileged to work with the now-famous 101st Airborne Division.

Eager to visit his Grandmother Baker, Darwin unpacked and took a trip to her home. Though he loved his mother, his grandmother was the most influential person in his life. She had ensured his participation in church, and he willingly attended for fear of disappointing her.

Before he had left for boot camp, she had presented him with a pocket-sized Book of Mormon made especially for military personnel. She counseled him to read from it each day, and he pledged to spend as much time as possible doing so.

Darwin kept his promise all through basic training, but when he began his Special Forces training, he didn't have the opportunity to continue his studies. Fearing the book would be lost or damaged, Darwin sent it to his grandmother for safekeeping. Now he was anxious to resume his reading and asked his grandmother for the book, which she promptly returned.

As they talked, she noted that Darwin's normally cheerful demeanor had changed to a nervous apprehension. He was clearly struggling to express a troubling thought. Finally, he began, "I don't know what it means for sure, but for the last six nights in a row, just before I came home, I kept having the same awful dream. I'm leading a patrol, and as I'm walking down the jungle path with trees all around it, all of a sudden, I come to a bend in the path. As I turn the corner, something really hard hits me in the chest, and I'm killed. When I wake up from my dream, my chest hurts—aches—for several minutes."

He continued describing the dream in detail, giving her the particulars of the surroundings, even the types of trees in the surrounding jungle. Obviously, the nightmare was still vivid in his mind, and his grandmother could tell he was upset as he recalled the details. Once he had finished explaining, he felt relieved, and half-joking, he finished, "So if I get shot, don't be surprised if I'm killed."

Sensing his uneasiness, his grandmother placed her hand over his.

"I promise you, Darwin, if you continue reading the Book of Mormon, you won't have to worry about your safety." She paused and then added, "I promise the Lord will take care of you." She stood and gently tugged him up. He bent his six-foot-nine frame and hugged her tenderly.

From that night on, he renewed his determination to keep his promise to his grandmother, drawing great comfort from her promise of protection.

***

When Darwin arrived in Vietnam, he had little time to adjust to life in a war zone and the humid climate of the tropics. Like most soldiers, he was immediately thrown into combat duty. His squad of Green Berets was frequently assigned to especially dangerous duties, and not more than a month after his arrival, Darwin found himself leading a patrol in an unfamiliar area reported to be heavily infiltrated by enemy snipers. They carefully and quietly inched their way down the heavily foliaged trail.

Suddenly, Darwin felt as if he were walking into a dream. It was eerily recognizable, though he knew he'd never been there before. In an instant, the terrifying dream was being played out in real life—the trees, the trail—it was all as he remembered. As he reached the bend in the path, a shot rang out, and his chest felt like it was on fire. The pain was overwhelming.

After about ten minutes, Darwin regained consciousness. He struggled to wake up from the confusion that enveloped his mind. He lifted his right arm and rubbed the soreness in his chest. He touched his left shirt pocket and noticed a hole. After unbuttoning the pocket, he removed two clips of ammunition and his Book of Mormon.

His hands still shaking from shock, he inspected the items. He saw a hole cut cleanly through both magazines. He also noticed that the bullet had pierced the back cover of his book. Flipping the book over, he found no hole in the front cover, and when he squeezed the book, he noted an unusual bump. Thumbing through the first few books, he carefully peeled the pages open and discovered the bullet lodged in the Book of Alma.

Gently prying the misshapen slug from the book, he discovered that it had penetrated over a hundred pages. The last page the bullet had pierced was page 305. He noticed a small hole seemingly marking the fourth verse of Alma chapter forty-four.

Amazed, he read the verse:

"*Now ye see that this is the true faith of God; yea, ye see that God will support, and keep, and preserve us, so long as we are faithful unto him, and*

*unto our faith, and our religion; and never will the Lord suffer that we shall
be destroyed except we should fall into transgression and deny our faith."*

He rubbed the slug mindlessly between his thumb and forefinger.
That bullet should have killed him, but he remembered his grandmother's
promise.

Later in the day, the captain of Darwin's unit came to visit him at the
field hospital. Darwin recounted the circumstances of his experience. The
captain just shook his head in disbelief, saying, "It's the most amazing
thing I've ever seen."

The captain then explained to Darwin that the Viet Cong sniper had
been no more than fifty feet from Darwin when he'd been hit. Additionally,
the sniper had used a long-barreled 7.92mm Mauser rifle, so powerful
that a version of it had been employed as an anti-tank weapon during
World War II. The ammunition used by the Viet Cong had been known
to pierce through three inches of steel from a hundred yards. Darwin was
not just lucky, he was undoubtedly blessed.

In a letter home, Darwin testified, "Someone must be looking out for
me. All I got from it was a heartache and a large bruise in my chest. I also
ripped my pants out in the seat when it knocked me down. I think that
it has taught me a lesson about the Church, and if I make it, I think that
you will see a difference in me."

Darwin was shortly returned to duty. He completed that tour and a
subsequent tour safely, and in 1968, he was awarded an honorable discharge.
He kept his Book of Mormon throughout his life, cherishing and protecting
it until his death in 2010. True to his word, he never forgot how fortunate
he was to be a witness of such an incredible phenomenon of God's love and
power. The book was a constant reminder of God's blessings, giving him
strength to endure the many struggles he faced throughout his life. Prior
to his passing, he arranged to have his bullet-riddled Book of Mormon
donated to the LDS Church History Library where it resides today.

SEEING THE HAND OF GOD
Matthew Barkdull

Pray! You haven't prayed about any of this. Trust that you will receive an answer.

Matthew almost heard the words as he sat alone in the house. His wife had gone outside to do some yard work, and the kids were off playing. He had decided to use the opportunity to clear the tumultuous thoughts bouncing around in his head. He was distraught and angry. He knew he should return to the hospital, but the thought of spending even more time away from his family was frustrating. He had been in the hospital only two weeks earlier. He was tired of being sick.

This rotting body is keeping me from my most basic desires, he thought. He only wanted to be a good husband and father. That was good, noble. Why couldn't God just let him be normal to fulfill those important roles? He was convinced his life was a failure. That's when the prompting came.

Pray.

Of course. Matt felt ashamed for not thinking of it sooner. He realized that maybe he didn't think the Lord could fix this particular problem. The power and persistence of this unrelenting health crisis had baffled medical science up to this point so surely not even God could fix this problem. Or could He? Could a simple prayer be that powerful?

Waving aside his doubts, Matt mustered up what faith he could from his near-empty spiritual reserves. He knelt down on the living room floor, his arms resting on the chair his grandmother had left him when she had passed away just a few months earlier.

He spoke aloud, asking forgiveness for his weak faith. "Lord, what should I do?" he continued. "Do I really need to go to the hospital again? None of this makes sense. And my family—what about them? I want to live. I can't imagine being away from them."

He paused. He didn't know what else to say. He had gotten to the heart of his struggles and didn't know how to proceed. Words just didn't seem enough to express the emotions he felt. So instead of praying out loud, he focused on pouring his heart out to the Lord.

Suddenly, he had the very subtle yet unmistakable feeling that he was being watched.

Had the kids come inside? he thought. He turned around and saw no one. Still, the feeling persisted. He closed his eyes, and a strong, warm sensation came over him. Someone *had* come into the room—his Grandpa Ralph, who died before Matt was born, and Grandma Georgia, only recently deceased. His natural eyes saw nothing, but his spiritual eyes saw the couple in their radiance. They delivered their message: "The hospital stay is the right thing. Do it and do it now!"

***

Matthew Dean Barkdull was born with a severe, genetic, blood-clotting disorder called hemophilia. Among other complications, the disease causes internal bleeding attacks that can be debilitating and even life-threatening if not treated quickly. Most hemophiliacs of his generation contracted either Hepatitis C or HIV, which led to AIDS. In fact, nearly 95 percent of his age group were diagnosed with HIV, so it was a miracle that Matt hadn't contracted that, though he was later diagnosed with Hepatitis C.

As if the hemophilia wasn't enough of a challenge, Matt suffered complete kidney failure at the age of fifteen. He had nearly died from the ordeal, but his father had once more bestowed the gift of life and donated a kidney to his son.

By age thirty-one, Matt was married and had three beautiful daughters, ranging in age from one to six. It was August when he began to hemorrhage internally. Although this kind of bleeding had occurred before due to his hemophilia, he couldn't escape the prompting that something wasn't right.

Matt called the doctor and explained his symptoms, sharing his fear that something was seriously wrong. His instincts were telling him it was related to his transplanted kidney, but he didn't want to believe that. Although medical specialists had explained the eventual failure of this kidney, deep down, Matt was determined to not allow himself to believe it would ever happen. He clung to his belief that God would intervene and prevent this precious organ from succumbing.

The doctor instructed Matt to start an IV of clotting medicine, but following that infusion, Matt was more certain than ever that something was not right. All indications were that the bleeding hadn't subsided but seemed to have worsened. Matt knew that by reporting these results, he would condemn himself to yet another hospital stay. He needed guidance and wasn't in an emotional state to make this decision without some measure of hope and consolation.

After his prayer and the message from his grandparents, Matt felt an indescribable peace wash over him. The Spirit was strong and further confirmed the answer he'd received. He needed to get to the hospital right away.

When he told his wife of the prompting, she related that she'd also received a confirmation that what he'd experienced was true: he needed to get to the hospital.

***

As soon as Matt arrived at the hospital, doctors began prepping him for surgery. They were going to remove the kidney. His symptoms were too severe for any other treatment. Matt realized what a tremendous blessing that kidney had been. It had served him for over sixteen years. It had allowed him to start a family and experience more life. Now it was causing serious complications. Matt knew it was necessary, but the thought saddened him.

The surgery went well, and a few days later while waiting to be discharged, Matt had visitors. The doctors came into his room and dropped a bombshell—the kidney they had removed was loaded with cancer. They had been doing a routine biopsy on the organ when the cancer was discovered.

Matt was stunned. The next few days were tense ones as he awaited word from the specialist to find out if they'd removed the kidney before the cancer had spread. Finally, the news came—the cancer was gone. Matt thought back to the urgent message he'd received from his grandparents. The longer he waited, the more likely it was that the cancer would have spread. He felt a surge of gratitude for the warning he'd received.

***

That wasn't the end of his problems though. Not even a week after his kidney had been removed, Matt began experiencing complications during a dialysis treatment. He tried to ignore the pain. Since he was still recovering from major surgery, he assumed that the discomfort was nothing serious.

He returned home, but by that time he could no longer ignore how awful he felt. His wife encouraged him to sit outside while she worked in the garden. She could keep an eye on him there, and the outside air might even help, she told him.

Reasoning that it couldn't hurt, Matt carefully stepped onto the porch and gingerly sat. He closed his eyes and tried to enjoy the sunshine, but unexpectedly, he felt a strange sensation come over him. It was a feeling he'd never had before. His whole body felt incredibly heavy, as if something was holding him down. Paradoxically, at the same time he felt weighed down, he began to feel detached from his body.

He couldn't comprehend what was happening. He opened his eyes, and a sudden surge of fatigue came over him. His body seemed to be powering down, one organ at a time shutting off. Matt realized how easy it would be to let his spirit depart. His previous brushes had never brought him this close to the veil.

With all the strength he could muster, he forced himself to stand. From the garden, his wife peered up at him. Matt returned her gaze. His eyes welled up, and he blinked back tears as he tried to explain, "I'm really sick."

Matt stumbled inside, praying that his will to live could overcome the physical approach of death. As he prayed, he had a calming thought come to his mind—*God has not brought me this far to fail.* It was at this moment that he resolved to do everything in his power to overcome this illness.

Matt asked his parents to bring him to the hospital so his wife could remain home with the children. They rushed over to pick him up and waited while Matt hugged his wife good-bye. He couldn't help but wonder if he'd ever see her and his children again. He could only hold on to the hope he'd gleaned from prior blessings.

Only moments after he arrived at the hospital, Matt's respiratory rate and oxygen levels plummeted. Acute respiratory failure.

Matt was moved to the intensive care unit, and the doctor explained the situation: "We can do nothing more except have a ventilator machine do the breathing for you. We'll insert a tube down your throat, and the machine will move air in and out of your lungs. We'll put a feeding tube through your nose so you can get proper nutrition while the ventilator is working. So your body will tolerate the ventilator, we'll induce a coma. When you're out of danger, we will wake you up. Do we have your consent to do all of this?"

Matt didn't see any other option. He agreed. He asked that they notify his wife before starting the procedure. As soon as she was notified, the medical staff bustled to and fro, preparing to begin the procedure. He lay still, watching them competently do their jobs, hoping that this would save his life.

At last, they placed a large plastic hood over his head. Initially, he struggled, gasping for breath. Matt began to panic until the strong flow of exquisite oxygen enveloped him. Ravenously, he inhaled, and the sweet air filled his lungs.

The last thing he heard were the doctor's words: "Don't worry, Matt. We'll take good care of you."

***

Nothing could compare to the intense and frightening sense of powerlessness he felt when the doctors brought Matt out of the coma. Panic was his first reaction as he attempted to breathe. With the tube still in his throat, he couldn't breathe. His gag reflex caused him to begin choking on the tube. Confused and alarmed, he tried to reach up and yank the tube out of his mouth. But the medical team had anticipated that natural tendency and had tied his hands to the sides of the bed.

His eyes opened wide in terror as he labored to inhale; however, he noticed that if he concentrated on breathing around his mouth and not his chest, it was easier to breathe. Relieved to have finally caught his breath, he looked around. A nurse stood next to him, holding his wrist. The nurse explained that Matt had been in a coma for two days.

Two days? He was astonished. It seemed as though mere seconds had elapsed from when he'd heard the doctor say he would take care of Matt. He couldn't recall a thing. No dreams, no stirring, nothing.

Another day passed before Matt finally got the news he'd been waiting for. A smiling nurse entered his room. "Your oxygen levels are looking fine now." Matt breathed a sigh of relief as she continued, "Let's get those contraptions out of your nose and mouth."

Matt seemed to be out of danger for the moment, but since they still weren't sure what had caused the respiratory system to fail, doctors kept him in intensive care where he would be more closely monitored.

The following day while Matt's wife and mother visited, the conversation turned to speculations about what had caused the respiratory failure. His mother told Matt that she had been impressed to do some research about what could have caused the problem. In the midst of this research, she had found an interesting possibility. Knowing it sounded implausible, she wanted to share her theory.

"Matt, I know this sounds a bit odd, but I've been thinking that many of your symptoms could have been caused by the West Nile virus."

Matt knew to trust his mother's instincts. Though the West Nile virus was quite rare, Matt requested that the doctors order the test. They were already drawing blood every day for various lab tests, so it was a simple request.

The medical staff was dubious to say the least. The virus didn't typically affect humans, but those with a compromised immune system *were* more likely to contract it. The doctor relented and ordered the test. A few days later, the Utah State Health Department confirmed that Matt did indeed have the West Nile virus. When the test came back positive, doctors and nurses were both astounded and enlightened. Everything began to make sense.

Finally, knowing the reasons for Matt's failing health, doctors were able to treat him more effectively. As the treatment changed, Matt's recovery accelerated beyond all expectations, and Matt was discharged from the hospital.

Later, as Matt made a routine visit to a medical specialist, the doctor marveled aloud, "Matt, you have been through the ringer." He paused before continuing. "Can I ask you something? Do you believe in miracles?"

A little surprised, Matt nodded his head, wondering where this was going.

"What would you say if I told you that the West Nile virus probably saved your life?"

Matt was utterly confused. He thought about those days of lying in the hospital bed, wondering whether he'd survive. He thought about the pain he'd endured and the moments of doubt and the fears of not seeing his little girls grow up. How could the virus that had almost killed him have saved his life? He just stared at the physician, waiting for the man to continue.

"I've been thinking about this. During the last several months, every doctor assumed that your symptoms were due to your failing kidney."

Matt nodded again. He could never forget how his grandparents' warning had gotten him into the hospital before the cancer in his kidney had been able to spread.

"Do you realize that most of the symptoms you were experiencing were from the virus and not from kidney failure? If you hadn't had those terrible symptoms, we never would have removed your kidney. Do you understand what I'm saying?"

Matt did.

"If we hadn't removed that kidney when we did, the cancer would have spread throughout your body. Once this type of cancer spreads beyond the kidney, radiation and chemotherapy are almost powerless against it. It would have been an almost guaranteed death sentence. West Nile gave you the symptoms that convinced us to remove your kidney. Without those symptoms, we would be having a very different conversation right now." The doctor looked Matt squarely in the eye. "You obviously have someone watching over you."

The Lord had made his presence and omnipotence known. What Matt had once thought to be a curse ended up being the Lord's way of saving his life. Everything now made sense. It was incredible how it all worked out, and a pervading, spiritual sensation swept over him.

"You're right," Matt finally told the doctor, knowing exactly who was watching over him.

BRONSON'S FATEFUL MOMENT

Sara Staker

Saturday, January 30, 2010

It started out like a typical Saturday. We just finished breakfast as a family, and my husband Matt had decided to take an unplanned mountain bike ride. He would probably be alone, but it was possible a friend could join him, depending upon his schedule.

My nine-year-old son, Kaden, was playing video games in our family room. My six-year-old, Trevan, was watching cartoons. As usual, my two babies, Daynen (two and a half) and Bronson (16 months), were a mess, covered in their breakfast. I had just come home from the gym. I needed a shower, and I usually took them with me. It was easier, faster, and less of a mess to shower them.

But just a couple weeks ago, they had their first actual bath together. They'd loved it! They'd splashed and laughed and played for hours! I thought I needed to take the time to let them do that more often. As we moved past the bath, Daynen begged to get in the "hot tub," our big, jetted bathtub in our bathroom. For once, we weren't in a hurry to go anywhere, so I started their water, put them in the tub with their toys, and set out their towels. I played with them a few minutes while the tub filled. I ran the water a few inches deep then turned off the faucet.

I poked my head around the corner into our bedroom to check on Trevan. He'd been sick the previous day. He looked skinny and cold and was shivering. I suggested he go get his pajamas on, but he said he was too tired.

And so I left, which turned out to be the biggest mistake of my life. I should never have walked away from that tub.

I grabbed Trevan's pajamas but got distracted by a couple of small, quick chores that I saw needed to be done. Suddenly, I heard a muffled shout, then Trevan came running, "Mom! Mom! Bronson drowned in the tub! I think he's dead!"

I ran, but the distance to the bathtub seemed like a mile. Bronson was floating on his back. His skin was white, lips blue, and eyes rolled back. He was gone.

Why was there so much water? It was up past the jets. Running at full speed. Somehow it was turned back on.

I screamed, "Kaden . . . call 911," but he was already there. Phone in hand. Dialing.

I began CPR. I blew air into my baby's lungs, and I watched as they filled and rose. I blew again, pleading with him, "Come on." He had no pulse. I pressed down on his chest, both hands shaking. Counting. Praying.

Any second . . . any second now his eyes would flutter, and he would take a breath. Any second now he would sit up. Any second now I would wrap my arms around him and thank God. Any second now he would be back with us.

Any second now . . . but he did not wake up.

Emergency responders arrived within minutes and whisked my baby out the door while I pleaded with them to save my baby.

Angels in the form of my neighbors appeared to tend my children so I could get to the hospital. A police officer escorted me to his car and drove me to see my little boy.

The drive was awful. We hit every light red on the mile and a half drive down the hill to the hospital. I wanted to get out and run.

At last, we made it, and I dashed through the doors of the emergency room, where I was ushered into a small, empty waiting room. That's when Matt came bursting through the door. I was stunned to see him. He had been on his bike. He shouldn't have been able to hear his phone. But he'd been waiting for a friend to call, so he'd been paying close attention to his phone. I was relieved not to have to go through this alone. His loving words lifted a weight off my shoulders.

Our bishop arrived quickly. He and Matt placed their hands on Bronson's little head and pronounced a priesthood blessing. We all wept. Matt voiced the blessing, and his words filled me with hope. He commanded Bronson to be made whole, then he called down the powers of heaven to preserve our son's life.

When the doctors had stabilized Bronson, the decision was made to transfer him via medical helicopter to Primary Children's Medical Center in Salt Lake City. We followed as quickly as we could via car.

By the time we arrived, Bronson's heart was beating on its own, but he was still not breathing without the ventilator. Since we didn't know how long he'd been underwater, we didn't know the extent of the damage. We did know that Kaden placed the 911 call at 11:20 and that Bronson had arrived at the hospital at 11:31. That was at least eleven minutes. We didn't know if he'd survive.

Sunday, January 31

We made it through the first torturous night. Neither Matt nor I slept well.

Bronson's early morning chest X-ray revealed fluid in his right lung. Doctors started him on an antibiotic to keep the pneumonia from worsening. We were encouraged by the results from a barrage of tests. He even came out of sedation enough to look around and blink, no doubt trying to make sense of where he was and what he was seeing.

Monday, February 1

The morning chest X-ray showed a more concentrated area of fluid. By the evening, doctors suspected that a portion of his lung had collapsed, and they made adjustments to prevent further damage.

The neuro-assesment proved to bring both good and bad news. Bronson was much less responsive and seemed more sluggish coming to. His pupils were still reactive but were unevenly dilated. On the other hand, we noticed that he was beginning to make eye contact. He also seemed to follow, or track, familiar voices.

We were still praying for our boy to recover fully. I hoped it wasn't too much to ask. Already, so many tender mercies had been extended. So many friends and family had texted, sent messages and gifts, called, and come to visit. Meals seemed to be coming in by the truckload. Our wonderful next-door neighbor, Jacque, already had meals coordinated through the next week. One came from our dear friend, Jane. She arranged to send us a meal from her vacation in Maui!

Tuesday, February 2

Bronson came to and made eye contact with both Matt and me. We were sure he recognized us! He looked around trying to figure out where he was. He made expressions. He looked worried. Confused. He scowled a little when something bugged him. He got good and mad at our nurse, Ian, when he didn't like the stimulus tests. He raised his arms up by his ears and shook his head while they scrubbed his head and combed his hair. He put on a darn good show, and we were all cheering like crazy!

We offered many prayers of gratitude that night!

Wednesday, February 3

One of our fabulous nurse practitioners, Erik, spoke to us. He compared recovery from a post-arrest neurotrauma to peeling an onion. When a child is so sick that he is on life-sustaining devices, you just slowly wean him off of one thing at a time. Then wait and see how he does. Then you go on to the next layer and work from there. We had many layers left to go, and we could only think about one at a time.

Friday, February 5

We were chasing out fear and choosing faith. The MRI was encouraging. There was nothing concrete, but at least it wasn't bad news.

I had left Bronson's room at about 4:30 in the morning to try to get a little sleep. Before I left, he'd opened his eyes, and our hearts had connected, but when I came back only a few hours later, something had changed.

I knew immediately when I walked into my son's room. The nurse filled me in. He told me that when he'd arrived on shift he assessed Bronson and found him a little sluggish, wide awake but not fully alert. He was staring blankly without focusing. He was unresponsive to stimulus. What had changed in that three hours and forty-five minutes? No one had an answer.

Our doctor explained that a neurotrauma injury can evolve and often plateau. Was this our plateau? Was this the boy we would be left with? We felt defeated. Like someone had just let the air out of our balloon.

Our stake president stopped by that day, and he and Matt gave Bronson another priesthood blessing. This one was harder for me to hear. Matt again spoke the blessing, turning the little body and soul back over to the God who had helped us create him.

They were able to squeeze Bronson in for an MRI that afternoon. The feeling I had was unmistakable. I knew Heavenly Father lives. I knew He loved Bronson and had a plan for his life. If it was God's will for him to remain with us, he would. It was as simple as that. I could not consider the other option. There was no other option.

Friday night was the first night I was alone. After my boys came to visit, Matt went home with them. He needed to be a daddy. Bless him.

I was up most of the night, cozied up in a corner recliner in B's room. I nodded off in the early hours of the morning until the night nurse came to tell me it was seven a.m. It was time for parents and visitors to leave the room for an hour during shift change and assessments. I hated that hour. It was misery to leave Bronson's bedside.

I did everything I could to pass those long minutes, then I looked at the clock. It was only 7:15. Only fifteen minutes had passed. Not knowing what else to do, I snuck into Bronson's room to get a blanket, then I wrapped myself up in a little cocoon and sunk down on the floor in the hallway to wait to be readmitted to the room.

The next thing I knew, Ian, the daytime nurse, was crouching above me on the cold tile floor. I had fallen asleep in the hallway outside Bronson's room. Ian was telling me to go to bed. At first, I just couldn't respond, but when I looked up into his eyes, the floodgates broke.

"Don't make me leave him! Please don't make me leave him! That's why we're in this mess in the first place! I just can't ever leave him!" I sobbed.

Ian literally scooped me up, wrapped me a little tighter in the blanket, and practically carried me down the hall to the parent sleeping cells, where Matt had been looking for me.

Saturday, February 6

It was a slow and quiet day for our little man. He was awake for most of the day but still had that blank empty stare that we hated. He had a couple of spontaneous breathing trials, where they turn the ventilator to standby mode and see how he does breathing on his own. We knew they would keep at it until Bronson could breathe without the machine.

Late in the morning, we had another scare. Bronson was having difficulty with his respirations, even on the ventilator. Some adjustments were made, and by noon, he seemed to be doing better.

Sunday, February 7

We attended a sacrament meeting at the hospital and returned to Bronson's room feeling spiritually nourished and strengthened. Bronson seemed to be doing well through another breathing trial, but as soon as it was over, he started having some trouble. His breathing was fast and hard, like he was breathing air through a straw. His heart raced, and he looked exhausted.

Late in the afternoon, I noticed his tummy looked a little too rounded. I pointed it out to the nurse, and she agreed. They used a large syringe to pull the trapped air from his stomach.

Tuesday, February 9

I wanted to shout it from the rooftops! "We have a modern marvel happening here in room 2314!" I was so excited that I could barely type my blog as it was happening. I was shaking. *Bronson was awake!*

Words could not express what I was feeling. He was in there after all. The lights were on!

Friday, February 12

We were told that Bronson could come home. They saw no reason to keep him. They'd discharged him from PICU the previous day but had wanted to watch his pneumonia one more night. He'd slept on my chest all night.

***

Bronson is here now. He is complete. Whole. Himself. Seemingly unaffected by all that happened. We know that his life was not just given to him, not even just to us. We believe it was given for the benefit of mankind. To show forth the all-powerful hand of God. To remind us that our loving Father in Heaven has a plan for us and for our families. That He hears and answers our prayers. That He intervenes, when necessary, to accomplish His will. That we were blessed enough to witness one of these occurrences firsthand.

EPILOGUE—AN INVITATION

FOR THOSE FEATURED IN THIS book, their lives were changed as a result of divine intervention. And while each story highlights a wonderful outcome, it's important to note that the lessons are not limited to just the thrill of an incredible story. I hope you will prayerfully seek out important lessons from these stories and apply them to your own life.

During the process of preparing this book for publication, I discovered how these uplifting stories can be used to teach important gospel principles. Interestingly enough, the Spirit can use the same story to teach each of us different lessons according to our needs.

This concept was pointed out to me by a close friend who is far more in tune with the Spirit than I am. She wrote to tell me what she learned from the story of Michael Dunn's bear attack:

"I love that we can focus on how Michael was able to follow the promptings of the Spirit to ultimately survive that ordeal. What I found incredibly interesting is that had he followed earlier promptings, he wouldn't have been in that situation at all. Now, I don't mean that as a criticism at all. Actually, it brings a great deal of comfort to me. The Lord warned Michael not to go, but even when he didn't follow those promptings, the Lord gave him more that ultimately saved his life. It is such a testament to the Lord's mercy. Even when we're too stubborn to listen the first time, he doesn't abandon us to our own devices. He is always there, extending a hand of mercy and love, just waiting for us to come to him."

Here's yet another insightful lesson pointed out to me by a friend after reviewing all the stories in this book:

"In order to experience a miracle, we have to need a miracle. I know that doesn't make sense, so let me explain. All of these people were in dire places. The stories focus so much on the good things that happen (as they should, I think)

that we forget how they must have felt in the moment. We tend to want to see miracles in our own lives, but we don't want the experiences necessary to require a miracle.

For example, I just finished Matthew Barkdull's story about all his health problems. I would imagine it would be easy to get wrapped up in the drudgery of suffering all those things. It would be easy to complain and doubt that the Lord was there. It would be easy to ask, "Why me?" I think these stories offer such a message of hope—that in our own lives, when things seem to be at their lowest point, that's when we can expect miracles. That's when we should be looking for miracles. Not everyone gets the miracle they want or expect, but if we're looking closely, we, like Matthew Barkdull, will eventually be able to look back and realize that everything happened for a reason."

As you can see, the Spirit can use miraculous stories to teach us important lessons that can help us deal with our own trials and circumstances.

This book features seventeen instances when God intervened to save one of His children. But these stories are just the tip of the iceberg when it comes to the number of uplifting and inspiring stories that exists. Maybe you have a story or know of one.

If you have witnessed the miraculous hand of God in your life, or know of someone who has, I invite you to prayerfully consider sharing your story. You may never know what lessons may be taught or whose life may be changed by hearing your story. I am always looking for new, uplifting stories for future projects, so please contact me via Facebook at www.Facebook.com/gtoyn, on Twitter at @GaryToyn, or via Covenant Communications at http://www.covenant-lds.com/contact.

Gary W. Toyn

ABOUT THE AUTHOR

GARY W. TOYN KNOWS A little about living dangerously, and he has the scars to prove it. When he was a baby, a broken window sliced his face, and he nearly bled to death. He was attacked by a deranged patient when he worked in a psychiatric hospital, and he walked away from a helicopter crash in the jungles of Honduras. Much less dangerously, he has worked as a lead singer in an eighties cover band, as a video producer, a journalist, and a sports reporter covering the NBA.

His travels have taken him around the globe to nearly fifty countries, where he has interviewed and written about political leaders, dissidents, and reformers. For his first book *The Quiet Hero* (2007), he teamed up with Bob Dole and Orrin Hatch to tell the story of George Wahlen, a World War II Medal of Honor recipient. His recent books are *Life Lessons From Fathers of Faith* (2011) and its companion *Life Lessons From Mothers of Faith* (2012), featuring notable Latter-day Saints like President Thomas S. Monson, Steve Young, Mitt Romney, Jane Clayson Johnson, and Jimmer Fredette.

He is a home teacher and serves in priesthood leadership in Clinton, Utah.